Stuart
Happy reading
~~To~~ gie 30-06-22

Africans and Racism in The Diaspora

Africans and Racism in The Diaspora

JOHN OGIE

OGBE ENTERPRISES

Lagos State, Nigeria

+447960421940, SS08064992758, 08152305426

Email:Johnogie69@yahoo.co.uk

© JOHN OGIE, 2014

ISBN: 978-1-5272-5246-2

Published in 2014

Printed by: Academy Press Plc. Lagos.

Dedication

It is very sad today to know worldwide that a lot of people do not realize that every human being remains the same before almighty GOD.

My creator opened this door of opportunity for me to write about segregation, discrimination, racism and prejudice perpetrated against Africans in the Diaspora. I thank almighty GOD for his benevolence to me especially in the areas of intellectual gift and financial empowerment.

I give almighty GOD my creator the glory for sparing my life to write this book. I dedicate this book to you–Oh LORD, this is your book. According to the holy scripture (the bible) book of Romans chapter 9 verse 16- "It is not of him that willeth, nor of him that runneth, but of GOD that sheweth mercy." The mercy of God is upon this book hence it will command waves and enjoy rave reviews world-wide. Rock of ages, Ancient of days, El-Iohim, El-Shaddai, My fortress and My tower, bless this book. Jehovah Nissi, Jehovah Rapha, Jehovah tsekenu, the Alpha and Omega, the Omnipotent, Omnipresent and Omniscience GOD, over to you.

I also want to dedicate this book to the memory of my maternal grandfather late Pa Okuomose Eghute who was a very kind hearted man while alive.

Finally this book is dedicated to all African brothers and sisters who at one time or the other suffered bouts of racism, racial profiling, series of physical and verbal attacks in the Diaspora.

Foreword

I was delighted to have been asked to write an introduction to this most enlightening book on racism in the Diaspora. Reading and hearing about racism suffered by our African kinsmen living in the Diaspora, I am moved to support the author to realize his vision to write a book about it.

The author is a noble, compassionate and brilliant academic. He is a man of style and panache. As far as I know there has never been any book around this topic that distils it into a prac-tical resource designed to support professionals like immi-gration services worldwide, foreign affairs ministries, anthro-pologists, human rights agencies, Law firms, etc in their day to day work.

Before leaving the shores of Nigeria the author was a so-cio- political analyst and commentator. In the 1980s he con-tributed a series of articles for publication to the Nigeria Observer newspaper in Benin City. You need to read this emotional and informative book for you to avail yourself of what Africans pass through as they sojourn abroad. I have certainly learned a lot from reading the manuscripts and would like to commend him for the intensive and extensive work that has gone into its preparation.

Good people will certainly support the author's views against racism. Even Martin Luther King Jnr alluded to this assertion when he made that famous declaration in his "I HAVE A DREAM" message to the American people. He postulated that nobody should judge another by the colour of his or her skin but by the content of his or her character.

A greater portion of this book is a synthesis of the author's experiences of racism abroad. It is my sincere hope that all who dip into the pages of this book will feel the urge to go beyond mere consultation. This book is an epitome of the knowledge of racism that the print and electronic media worldwide spontaneously report and cry about.

I cherish the style and simple language used. The layout is superb. I love the inclusion of much unexpected materials, such as maps, photographs and other resources of great value. It is a valuable educative and informative book to read.

EMMANUEL IGBINIHOKHO

London, United Kingdom

2014

Preface

Racism has to do with the problem of acceptance of a certain race by another race. We have to admit that there is racial profiling and racial stereotype of Africans in the Diaspora. Racial discrimination of Africans is so acute that it has attracted attention and condemnation worldwide.

I decided to write about this cankerworm "RACISM" because of my personal nightmarish experiences. If I hadn't sojourned abroad, I would not be able to phantom the magnitude of the scourge. But experience is more impressive than hearsay.

A book of this sort is wonderfully an egalitarian and humanitarian work. This book will definitely intrigue people. I wrote this book to make statements - to expose racism, cry for compassion, plead for tolerance and proffer solutions to the menace.

In the opening chapters, definitions of major terms which appeared abstract were tied wherever possible to explanation that the reader can easily make sense of. Every comment, statement, map, picture and data used to form this book were thoroughly verified as accurate prior to publication.

The urgent need for a work of this character has been long overdue. All manners of African people sojourned abroad. Some remained while others returned back to mother Africa. A lot suffered and some are still suffering racism. All classes of people are affected students, clergy men and women, professionals in various fields like engineers, lawyers, pharmacists, nurses, midwives, accountants, sportsmen and women, asylum seekers, etc.

Unfortunately up till the time of writing this book no African brother or sister who sojourned abroad and suffered racism could write his or her experiences in the form of a book of this class. I could not phantom why it did not occur to them.

I felt that there is a huge vacuum created by the non existent of a book that deals on this title. So I rose up to the occasion when it dawned on me to write on it. Although, this book has consumed an excessive time in preparation, I am satisfied that the void has been filled with the publication of this incisive book.

The teacher in me is aptly displayed throughout the course of writing this book. I am able to educate and enlighten the whole world that racism sickens the body and mind. That it is ungodly, inhuman and obnoxious; and that it should be wiped out of the face of this lovely world. This is a pioneer book that has espouse racism causes, effect and solution.

Apart from my personal experiences, the composition of this book was enriched substantially by conversation with fellow African political asylum seekers at various political refugee camps across Europe. At various occasions, functions, meetings, parties, etc we had the opportunity to vent our anger against constituted authorities that fester institutionalised racism on immigrants, especially the Africans.

Been-to's and would be been-to's would want to know more about this subject. This book is written to satisfy the curiosity of these groups of people. The decision to write this book was a very easy one but writing a book is never easy. Having suffered racism in various places e.g. job place, on the streets, in the buses, in the trains, etc. I vowed that I should one day put all my travails into writing which culminated in writing this book.

It has been my aim to give as correct a picture as possible of what I experienced.

I know that a free-flowing style, a lively title, some well selected pictures and a striking paper back cover will often result in ample sales and uncritical readers. I strived to make all those qualities to bear on this book. Writing a book like this is a little like building one's own house. One not only creates something but uses it every day, takes pride in its construction and lives with it and inside of it for the rest of ones life.

One of the pleasures of writing this book has been the knowledge that it focuses on a topic (racism) that affects the lives of every prospective African, yearning to travel abroad, and Africans already living in the Diaspora.

Right from the definition chapter, readers are availed with precise definition of key words that form the title of the book. Words like racism; Africa, Abroad or the Diaspora, etc. Thereafter the readers are taken through a series of episodes of racism experienced by me, right from the day I set my foot on the soil of Europe 23 Years ago - from Germany through Switzerland, the Netherlands to Belgium. It is my belief that the knowledge derived from this book, will be rewarding to the reader.

JOHN OGIE

London, United Kingdom
2014

Contents

CHAPTER ONE
The Concept of Racism

A s an introduction, it would be expeditious to define the major key words that combine to form the theme of this book. They are [i] RACISM [ii] AFRICANS [iii] ABROAD or DI- ASPORA. Definitions do not exist in the abstract, they serve specific purposes and objectives. Key among the objectives, is that it enable the reader understand the words and terms frequently used to explain ideas and concepts in the work.

RACISM - The Oxford English dictionary, second edition, volume X11 defines racism as the distinction of human characteristics and abilities by race. Racism refers to a doctrine of racial supremacy. Racism is a newer term for the word racialism. The Vatican radio often say that racism might have different faces but it will always be reprehensible.

Webster's third new international dictionary defines race as a group of human beings recognising a common history and common culture, yearning for a common destiny and generally attached to a specific piece of the earths surface.

J.R.Green defines race as any large group of people crossing national boundaries and with something significantly in common.

Edit Sitwel see racism as a body of persons as a whole or as individuals who show a consciousness of solidarity of common characteristics, suggesting a common culture or common interests or ideals and a sense of kinship.

Race is a word used to designate one of a number of great divisions of mankind, each made up of an aggregate of persons who think of themselves as comprising a distinct unit.

Race in anthropological and ethnological term imply a distinct physical type with certain unchanging characteristics e.g. Caucasian race, Malay race, etc. In popular use, race can apply to any more or less clearly defined group thought of as a unit because of a common or presumed common past e.g. Anglo-Saxon race, Celtic race, the Hebrew race, etc.

RACISM- The assumption that psycho-cultural traits and capabilities are determined by biological race and that races differ decisively from one another is usually coupled with a belief in the inherent superiority of a particular race and its right to dominate over others. Racism instigates hatred, rivalry or bad feeling between races. Racism fuels belief in the inherent superiority of a particular race over others. Discriminatory treatment are usually based on such a belief.

The object of discussion is Africa and Africans and the impact of racism on their way of life. Africa is the second largest continent, a southward projection of the old world landmass divided roughly in two by the equator and surrounded by sea except where the Isthmus of Suez joins it to Asia.

Africa is the second largest continent bordered by the Mediterranean in the north, the Atlantic in the west and south and the red sea, Gulf of Aden and Indian Ocean in the east. The Sahara desert divides the continent unequally into North Africa, an early centre of civilisation in close contact with Europe and West Asia, now inhabited chiefly by Arabs, and South Africa relatively isolated from the rest of the world until the 19th century and inhabited chiefly by Negroid people.

2

It was colonised mainly in the18th and 19th centuries by Europeans and now comprises independent nations. The largest lake is Lake Victoria and the chief rivers are the Nile, Niger, Senegal, Congo, Orange, Limpopo and Zambezi.

Its population is 755,919,000 approx (1998 estimate). The area is about 30,300,000 sq km or 11,7000,000 sq miles. Webster's third new international dictionary unabridged defines Africans as individuals of immediate or remote African ancestry especially the Negro. According to 0xford dictionary of English Africans are persons from Africa. English dictionary therefore defines Africans as denoting or relating to Africa or any of its peoples, languages, nations, etc - a native, inhabitant, or citizen of any of the peoples of Africa.

ABROAD- Longman contemporary English new edition defines 'abroad' as a foreign country. This means the spreading of people from a national group or culture to other areas.

Chambers dictionary large print new edition defines Diaspora as the dispersion of people of the same nation or culture.

Diaspora is a word of Greek origin. It derives from the Greek word. 'Diaspeirein'- **Dia** means across, **Speren** -means scatter or disperse.The term Diaspora originated from the Septuagint. Septuagint is the Greek version of the Hebrew bible (old testament). It originated from the Latin Septuaginta-meaning 'seventy' because it was produced by seventy-two translators.

So the term Diaspora means dispers, or movement to various locations, which originated in Septuagint (Deuteronomy 28:25), in the phrase - "ese diapora en pasais basileias te ges", meaning "thou shalt be a dispersion in all kingdoms of the earth."

The afore stated definitions and explanations of key words is to enable the reader to have an in-depth knowledge of the meaning of the title of this book-AFRICANS AND RACISM IN THE DIASPORA.

CHAPTER TWO

The Description of
the African Continent

Africa is the second largest continent, a southward two by the equator, and surrounded by sea except where the Isthmus of Suez joins it to Asia. The second largest of the continents is bordered by the Mediterranean in the north, the Atlantic in the west and the Red sea, Gulf of Aden and Indian Ocean in the east. In the south, it is also bordered by the Atlantic Ocean.

It was colonised mainly in the 18th and 19th centuries by Europeans and now comprises independent nations. The largest lake is lake Victoria. The chief rivers are the Nile, Niger, Senegal, Congo, Orange, Limpopo and Zambezi. The continent is hostile and filled with pests that endengers both man and animals. The peopling of an environmentally hostile continent meant Africans have been pioneers in the struggle against disease and nature. Their social, economic and political institutions have been designed to ensure survival. Suffering has been a central part of African experience, whether it arose from the harsh struggle with nature or the cruelty of men through slavery and colonisation. In presenting the history or description of Africa, adequate coverage is given to the physical, political, economic and human themes.

PHYSICAL GEOGRAPHY OF AFRICA

Africa straddles the equator extending almost as far south as it does north. This simple geographical fact is the basis for understanding the symmetrical distribution of African climates, vegetation and peoples on either side of the equator. Africa comprises a single tectonic plate. Almost the entire continent is a geologically stable landmass of Precambrian basement rocks partly overlain by later sedimentary cover.

In the extreme south-west corner, the fold mountains are of Hercynian age, in the extreme north-west the Atlas fold mountains are of the Alpine Orogeny. Elsewhere the stability is broken only by the rift valley system. In contrast to Europe, the continent of Africa has a remarkably smooth outline. Its coastline is short in relation to its area and there are few major inlets or peninsulas.

On a smaller scale there is a marked absence of natural harbours. The continental shelf of Africa again in contrast to Europe, is almost uniformly narrow. The absence of a wide continental shelf limits fishing opportunities and reduces the chances of finding oil fields. Africa has relatively few offshore islands and most are small and of volcanic origin.

The ocean currents off the African coast are influenced by the continent straddling the equator. Plains cover thousands of square miles, stretching away seemingly endlessly in a largely featureless landscape. The plateau consists of a number of vast shallow basins separated often by barely discernable watersheds. Occasionally, there are mountainous tracts of considerable watersheds. Rainfall is the climatic factor of greatest significance in Africa. Most of the continent has a small range of temperature, and wind is also much less of a feature than in temperate latitudes. Africa extends little beyond 35 degrees of latitude from the equator, thus limiting the range of African climates.

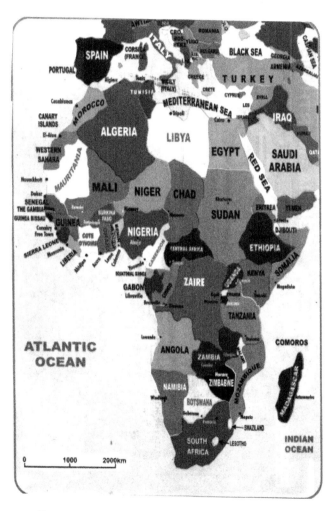

Africa really is the continent of sunshine and storm. Climatic conditions in many parts of Africa are severely trying for humans. The monotony of heat, humidity and daily climatic regime in humid, tropical areas is profoundly enervating. Many parts of Africa are periodically subjected to torrential rain, flood and devastation. African soils are highly varied -- a poor resource which is likely to deteriorate dramatically under pressure from increasing population. Soil erosion is already a widespread problem. Drought is endemic in the semi-arid desert fringes of Africa.

POLITICAL GEOGRAPHY OF AFRICA

The states of modern Africa are essentially colonial creations transformed into independent states. Their boundaries, shapes and sizes are part of the colonial inheritance. Mainland Africa has 46 independent states and 2 independent territories. There are 6 independent island states and 7 dependent island groups. According to the "great game of scramble", a European power first had to establish a claim to its stretch of African coastline and was then able to declare as its legitimate sphere of influence territory directly inland. The length of coastline claimed depended on how near on either side of its own trading post was to the next post of another European power. The total area of Africa is over 11.5 million sq miles (30 million sq km).

Thirty-one African states have an area greater than that of the United Kingdom. Only 2, Nigeria and Egypt have a greater population. For a variety of reasons, mostly originating in the colonial past, many independent African states are very small according to a number of criteria. Their extreme lack of size brings into question their economic and political viability and renders them peculiarly vulnerable to the forces of neo-colonialism.

ECONOMIC HISTORY OF AFRICA

By any material measure, in general the people of Africa are poor. The total GNP of all 52 states of Africa in the year 2000 was only about 7% of that of the United States of America according to the Guardian newspaper (UK) October 16, 2002. Not only do these figures represent a shocking poverty gap, but it is a gap which has grown dramatically wider in the last decade.

Nevertheless, there is no escaping from the assertions that, in material terms, Africa is a poor continent and that the poverty gap between Africa and industrialised countries as represented by the United States of America is widening rapidly. The poorest states in Africa are generally in the Sahel and the Horn, but the poorest of all is Mozambique. Somalia, Uganda, Ethiopia, Chad, Liberia, Sudan, etc, are war ravaged countries and there is a direct causal relationship between war and poverty, poverty and war, a vicious circle of human suffering. The poorest states also have few natural resources and have been hit repeatedly in recent years by natural disasters, ranging from crippling drought to devastating cyclones.

Non-manufacturing industry (mainly mining, including oil and gas exploitation) accounted for 20% or more of GDP in no fewer than 12 African countries. Manufacturing is the least developed. African countries depend heavily on the industrialised world for imports of manufactured products and increasingly lose out as the terms of trade consistently move in favour of manufacturers and against raw materials.

HUMAN GEOGRAPHY OF AFRICA-THE PEOPLE OF AFRICA

Human geography of Africa encompasses the social and cultural activities of the people of Africa. The total population of Africa according to United Nations estimates, probably exceeds 700 million people. The continent has an average population density of about 17 per sq km. Population growth rates in several African countries are now among the highest in the world and are undermining economic achievement by exceeding rates of economic growth.

The distribution of population is far from uniform. Three vast areas: the Sahara, the Kalahari and Namibian deserts, and the tropical rainforest of the Zaire (Congo) basin, support very small populations for obvious reasons. Up to 2000 languages are spoken today in Africa, which displays a greater degree of overall complexity than any other continent. Language groups are often divided between states.

Although slowly improving, low literacy rates are common throughout Africa. Emphasis is wrongly placed on academic rather than technical subjects. Impediments to human development include apartheid, cross-border conflicts, ethnic upheavals and civil strife. All of these result in 20 million refugees and 80 million disabled people whilst a further 60 million people are displaced through natural disasters and difficult economic conditions.

The main tribes of Africa are: the Swahilis, the Hausas, the Fulanis, the Mandingos, the Temne Mende people, the Bantus, the Zulus, the Ibos, the Yorubas, the Binis, the Kanuris and the Berbers. Eventually, the colonial governments imposed their foreign languages and culture on the people. As a result, the official languages used in the countries of Africa such as English, French, Portuguese, Italian, Dutch (Afrikanaar), etc. are a direct consequence of colonial contacts, meddling and hangover.

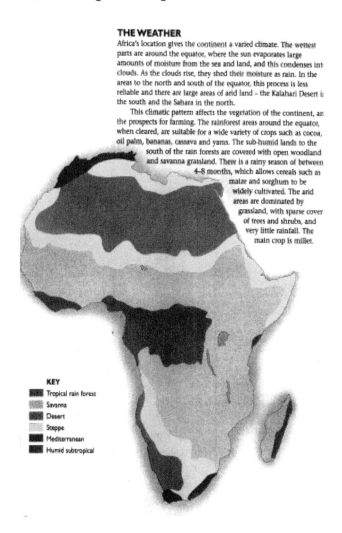

THE WEATHER

Africa's location gives the continent a varied climate. The wettest parts are around the equator, where the sun evaporates large amounts of moisture from the sea and land, and this condenses into clouds. As the clouds rise, they shed their moisture as rain. In the areas to the north and south of the equator, this process is less reliable and there are large areas of arid land – the Kalahari Desert in the south and the Sahara in the north.

This climatic pattern affects the vegetation of the continent, and the prospects for farming. The rainforest areas around the equator, when cleared, are suitable for a wide variety of crops such as cocoa, oil palm, bananas, cassava and yams. The sub-humid lands to the south of the rain forests are covered with open woodland and savanna grassland. There is a rainy season of between 4–8 months, which allows cereals such as maize and sorghum to be widely cultivated. The arid areas are dominated by grassland, with sparse cover of trees and shrubs, and very little rainfall. The main crop is millet.

KEY
Tropical rain forest
Savanna
Desert
Steppe
Mediterranean
Humid subtropical

THE PEOPLE OF AFRICA

CHAPTER THREE
Why the Migration from Africa

There are remote and immediate causes of emigration of Africans to the Diaspora.

REMOTE CAUSES
As Africa was a cradle of humankind so was Egypt the cradle of civilization. For 250 years, Africans were kidnapped and taken for slavery. During slave trade era, African Kings and traders captured and herded away their kinsmen in exchange for adulterated Brandy and Rum. African slaves were bought with expired bags of salt, second hand Caps, Swords, Knives, Axe-heads, Hammers, Mirrors, Belts, Bracelets, Iron Jugs, Rum, Guns, Gunpowder, e.t.c. During the slave trade era, Africans came to believe themselves to be inferior. They lost confidence in themselves, their culture and their ability to develop.

Slavery scarred the soul and wounded the spirit of Africans. Slavery hangover devastated the psyche of the Africans. Africans were socially disadvantaged because of the un-healed wound that was inflicted on them across the early centuries. They were psychologically crippled people which accounts for their current inferior position.

It was during the slave trade and slavery that white people affirmed their superiority over Africans. It is not difficult to understand why white traders bought black Africans for a price of adulterated brandy and packed them onto slave ships like cattles. They considered themselves to be superior.

After the abolition of slave trade, Africans were subjugated through colonialism and imperialism. During the first and second world wars, able bodied Africans were conscripted and shipped away to fight opponents of their colonial masters.

During and after the two world wars, African war veterans and ex-soldiers that fought for their colonial masters intermarried with white ladies and produced children of Semi-African stork. Berlin conference of 1884/1885 balkanised Africa among 13 European powers to guaranty a source of raw materials for their industries and provide markets for their arms and ammunitions. Africa natural resources were plundered and as a consequence suffered depletion in the hands of unrestrained European invaders.

The Benin punitive expedition (Benin massacre) of 1897 was a case in point. The simple fact that Oba Ovoranmwen vehemently resisted the take over of his trading routes by the Europeans led to the launch of an assault on his kingdom. During the mayhem, precious works of Art and Artefacts of cultural and historical interest that worth billions of Dollars were looted and carted away with impunity. The all powerful and glorious Benin Kingdom was sacked and its mansions were razed to the ground. Oba Ovoranmwen "no gbaisi" was forcefully deported to Calabar.

Anioma (Ogwashi - Uku) people of Delta state, Nigeria had one destiny prior to the coming of the Europeans. They were balkanized after they lost the **EKUMEKU WAR** of resistance against British imperialistic and exploitative rule in 1914. The war lasted 31 years. The **EKUMEKU WAR** was the longest resistance against British imperialism and bastardization of Nigeria. On loosing the war, the Europeans descended on the human and natural resources. These resources were plundered and thus suffered huge depletion.

● Areas of violence in Africa

Jaja of Opobo named Jubo Jubogha by the British who later took the name Jaja for his dealings with the British was another victim of imperialism. He was very agile. He was nick-named Jaja because of his business agility. His real name was Mbanaso Okwaraozurumba. He was the third son of Mr and Mrs Okwaraozurumba and was born at Umuduruoha, Amaigbo in 1821. He was an Igbo slave.

This gifted and enterprising individual eventually became one of the most powerful men in eastern Niger Delta. He rose to be the head of Anna Pepple house after the death of Anni of Bonny. This was the era of Gun Boat diplomacy where Great Britain used her naval power to negotiate condition favourable to the British. Unknown to Jaja the scramble for Africa had taken place and Opobo was part of the territories allocated to Great Britain. For resisting the British, he was arrested and sent to Accra for trial. Defenseless Jaja was found guilty and hurriedly deported to St.Vincent in West Indies.

In 1888, Prince Prempeh 1 ascended to the throne. He assumed the throne name Kwaku Dua 111. He refused to accept British protectorate over his Kingdom of Ashanti. The British even requested Ashanti people to turn over the golden stool which is the very symbol of Ashanti Monarchy. They resisted. Asantehene Prempeh 1 was exiled to Seychelles in the Indian Ocean area.

Aforementioned African traditional rulers gave themselves up for deportation because of the superior fire power of the Europeans. The traditional rulers were forcefully removed from their dormains to pave way for massive looting and unhindered plundering of the natural and human resources which subsequently engineered poverty. Similar ruthless scenarios played out across the African Continent.

IMMEDIATE CAUSES OF EMIGRATION: PUSH FACTORS

Many reasons led to emigration of Africans to Europe. Major among the reasons are the following: Poverty, lack of work, HIV/ AIDS, corruption in high places, and bad governance are among major issues that drive Africans from their homes and onto often tiny fishing boats to contend with the Atlantic ocean on their way to foreign lands.

In addition to the above push factors, uprising like that of the MAU-MAU revolt in Kenya, Civil wars in Namibia, Nigeria, Angola, Mozambique, the Congos, Western Sahara, Ogaden region , Guinea Bissau and Guinea Conakry, Liberia, Sierra Leone, Ivory Coast, Sudan, Ruanda, Burundi, etc. have devastated the regions of Africa in the past decades.

Desertification, Famine, Flood disaster, educational pursuit and the urge to play professional sports abroad are the other push factors. Poverty has taken hold of the majority of people in countries such as Senegal, Chad, Niger and Mali despite their relative peace and democracy.

At this juncture, it is very necessary to further explore the above mentioned push factors that conspired to force Africans to flee to other Continents.

MAU MAU UPRISING

Under the leadership of Mzee Jomo kenyata, Dedan Kimathi, Waruhiu Itote popularly known as General China, Tom Mboya, etc. Africans combined to fight off imperialistic oppression. Opposition against British colonial rule in Kenya culminated in the Mau Mau uprising which began in 1952. The Land of Kenya was raped and the people were psychologically destroyed. Thousands of citizens fled the country. However, the returning Kenyan soldiers that fought in the second world war helped to liberate the country.

NAMIBIA WAR OF INDEPENDENCE

The Namibia War of Independence which lasted from 1966 to 1988 was a guerrilla war which the nationalist South West Africa People's Organisation (SWAPO) under the leadership of Sam Nujoma fought against the apartheid regime of South Africa. Bearded Samuel Daniel Shafiishuna Nujoma otherwise known as Sam Nujoma was the leader of South West Africa People's Organization (SWAPO). During the struggle, Nujoma took the combat name "Shafiishuna", meaning lightening. On August 26, 1996 SWAPO guerrilla forces launched an attack against the South Africa Defence Force at Omugulugwombashe. A lot of lives were lost. Many citizens fled abroad.

NIGERIA-BIAFRA CIVIL WAR 1967-1970

The Nigerian federation united three major ethnic groups and about 250 smaller minor ethnic groups. Under the British colonial tutelage, it developed reasonably work-able political cohesion and promising economic prospects through five years of independence. But the corruption of first generation politicians triggered a coup that was led by Major Kaduna Nzeogu. The coup plotters were young army officers mostly Ibos from Eastern Nigeria.

The other military officers that participated in the execution of the coup were Major Tim Onwuatuegwu, Major Emmanuel Ifeajuna, Major Adewale Ademoyega and Captain Nwobosi (he was yet to be commissioned an Army Major). The tribal implications of that coup triggered in turn a sequence of assasinations, tribal atrocities and polarization culminating in the Eastern Nigeria's secession as "BIAFRA" and subsequently, the outbreak of war.

General Gowon led a fragile, relatively moderate and regionally balanced coalition determined to preserve national unity. The military governor of the Igbo dominated southeast, Colonel Odumegwu Ojukwu, citing the northern massacres and electoral fraud, proclaimed the secession of south-eastern region from Nigeria and renamed the area as the Republic of Biafra, an independent nation on 30 May, 1967. However, the Nigerian government launched a "Police action" to retake the secessionist territory. The war began on 6 July 1967. The war cost the Igbos a great deal in terms of lives, money and infrastructure. It has been estimated that up to three million people died due to the conflict. Thousands of people fled the country.

ANGOLAN CIVIL WAR
The Angolan Civil war was a major civil conflict in the African state of Angola, beginning in 1975 and continuing, with some interludes, until 2002. It began immediately after Angola became independent from Portugal in November, 1975. The civil war was primarily a struggle for power between two former liberation movements, People's Movement for the Liberation of Angola (MPLA) and the National Union for the Total Independence of Angola (UNITA). At the same time it served as a surrogate battleground for the cold war.

IMPLA was supported by Romania, Cuba and Soviet Union. UNITA, founded by Jonas Savimbi received support from China, USA and the state of South Africa. The 27 years civil war became one of the longest, bloodiest and most prominent armed conflicts of the cold war period. More than 500,000 people were killed and over one million people were internally displaced. Hundreds of thousands of people were amputated through landmines.

The war devastated Angola infrastructure, and dealt severe damage to the nation's public administration, economic enterprise and religious institutions. Tens of thousands of refugees created by the war are now in Angola and other parts of the world.

MOZAMBIQUE CIVIL WAR
Mozambique Civil war began in 1977, two years after the end of the war of independence. The ruling party, Front for Liberation of Mozambique (FRELIMO) and the national armed forces (Armed forces of Mozambique) FAM was violently opposed from 1977 by the Rhodesian and (later) South African funded Mozambique Resistance Movement (RENAMO). About one million people died in fighting and from starvation, and five million civilians were displaced. Many citizen fled. Many that fled abroad landed more in Portugal. Many after the war were made amputees by landmines, a legacy from the war that continues to plaque Mozambique.

THE WAR IN CONGO BRAZAVILLE
The civil war in the republic of Congo took place from June, 1997 to December 1999, and was fought between two presidential candidates. The war ended in an invasion of Angolan forces and installation of Denis Sassou Nguesso to power. This war is commonly known as the War of 5, June. It is a conflict that destroyed or damaged much of the Capital, Brazzaville.

Alongside the political conflict between Lissouba and Sassou Nguesso, oil was considered a crucial factor in the war, and with French interest at stake, France was seen as backing Sassou Nguesso against Lissouba. The conflict closed the economically vital Brazzaville-Point-Noire rail-road. It caused great destruction and loss of life in Southern Brazzaville. Displaced hundreds of thousands of persons and many citizens fled the country. Many that fled to overseas landed in Portugal.

WAR IN THE DEMOCRATIC REPUBLIC OF CONGO
The first Congo War (1996-1997) was started with a foreign invasion of Zaire led by Rwanda that replaced a decade's long dictator, Mobutu Sese Seko. The rebel leader was Laurent Desire Kabila. The second Congo war began in August, 1998 and officially ended in July 2003. The conflict in the Democratic Republic of Congo is sometimes known as Africa's first world war.

The fighting involved seven neighbouring nations at one time or another. Ruanda, Uganda, Zimbabwe, Namibia and Angola have all been involved. It has proved to be the planet's deadliest conflict since world war II. There are many militia groups and local warlords involved but the two main protagonists are the Congolese Army (FRDC) and the Democratic Forces For The Liberation of Rwanda (FDLR) rebels.

The Lord's Resistance Army (IRA) have also sought refuge in eastern Congo and have fought against the government troops. The vast mineral resources is what keeps the conflict going. War lords sell mineral resources to western buyers. They use the proceeds to fuel the war. More than 5.4 million people have died as a result. Sexual violence are perpetrated against little girls and women. Millions of Congolese have fled abroad. Many live in French speaking countries of France and Belgium. Others dwell in Canada and other western countries.

WESTERN SAHARA CONFLICT

Western Sahara conflict or Polisario Front dispute for independence is an ongoing conflict between the Polisario Front of the Sahrawi people and the state of Morocco.

The conflict is the continuation of the past insurgency by Polisario against the Spanish colonial forces in 1973-1975 and the subsequent Western Sahara war between the Polisario and Morocco (1975-1991). The conflict escalated after the withdrawal of Spain from the Spanish Sahara in accordance with the Madrid accords. Beginning in 1975, the Polisario Front, backed by Algeria and Libya waged a 16 year long war for independence against Mauritania and Morocco.

Following the annexation of Western Sahara by Morocco and Mauritania in 1976, and the Polisario Front's declaration of independence, the UN addressed the conflict via a resolution reaffirming the right to self determination of the Sahrawi people. Western Sahara conflict has resulted in severe human rights abuses, most notably is the bombardment of the refugee camps with white phosphorus.

These have resulted in exodus of tens of thousands of Sahrawi civilians from their country and the forced expulsion of tens of thousands of Morocco expatriates by the Algerian government. As a resulted somewhere on 14,000-21,000 casualties were recorded between both sides. Some 40, 000-80,000 Sahrawi refugees were displaced as a result of the conflict. At present, most of the refugees still resides in various Sahrawi refugee camps throughout the Tindouf province of Algeria. Tens of thousands of refugees have fled to France and Spain.

OGADEN REGION WAR

This was a border war between Ethiopia and Eritrea. American funded and Russian armed Ethiopian military doubled the size of its armed forces to fight in the 1998-2000 war against Eritrea. Italy backed Eritrea. Eritrea sustained 19,000 casualties in combat. Though the Eritreans were outnumbered and outgunned, abandoned and finally betrayed but they eventually won the war. They won by force of character, unity and determination so steely that the superior forces of Ethiopia could not withstand them. The final result of the border war came in the court room, where Eritrea was rewarded. Tens of Thousands of refugees produced by this war emigrated to Italy and some neighbouring African countries.

CIVIL WARS IN SUDAN:
THE FIRST SUDANESE CIVIL WAR

The first Sudanese civil war was known as the Anyanya rebellion, after the name of the rebels. It was a conflict from 1955 to 1972 between the northern part of Sudan and Southern Sudan region that demanded representation and more regional autonomy. Half a million people died over the 17 years of war. Tens of Thousands of refugees fled.

However, the agreement that ended the first Sudanese civil war in 1972 failed to completely dispel tensions that had originally caused it. Leading to a re-igniting of the North-South conflict.

SECOND SUDAN WAR (1983-2005)

The war is seen as a fight between the central government expanding and dominating people of the periphery, raising allegations of marginalisation. Some paint the conflict as racial (Arabs in the Central government versus Africans in the South), or as religious (Muslims versus Christians and Traditional African Religions). Exploitative governance is the root cause of the war.

The British did not help matters. After decolonisation, most of the powers was given to the northern elites based in Khartoun, causing unrest in the South. The second Sudanese war which originated in Southern Sudan, spread to the Nuba mountains and the Blue Nile. It lasted 22 years and roughly million people died. Millions of refugees were created by the war.

LIBERIA WAR

The Liberian civil war was an internal conflict in Liberia from 1989-1996. The second Liberia civil war started in 1999 and ended in 2003. Samuel Doe had led a coup de 'etat that overthrew the elected government of President William R. Tolbert Jr. in the executive mansion. Doe was a part of a rural Krahn tribe. It was a minority group. A civil war began in December, 1989 when rebels intent on toppling Doe entered Liberia through Cote d' Ivoire. Doe's forces were defeated and in September, 1990 he was captured, totured and executed. The first Liberia civil war killed over 200,000 people. Many fled the country to neigbouring African countries. Tens of thousands are scartered in the Diaspora.

In 1999 Charles Taylor who had left Doe's government after being accused of embezzlement assembled a group of rebels in Cote d' Ivoire (mostly, ethnic Gios and Manos who felt persecuted by Doe). The group was known as the National Patriotic Front of Liberia (NPFL). By middle of 1990 a civil war was raging. Taylor's NPFL soon controlled much of the country while Prince Johnson who splitted from Taylor began advancing into the capital, Monrovia.

The second Liberia civil war began in April 1999, when Liberia dissidents under the banner of the Organization of Displaced Liberians invaded Liberia from Guinea. Tens of Thousands were killed and maimed. Many fled to other African countries. Scores of the refugees made it to Europe and the Americas. Charles Taylor forces was defeated and he was exiled to Nigeria.

SIERRA LEONE'S CIVIL WAR (1991-2002)
The war began on 23 March, 1991 when the Revolutionary United Front (RUF) with the support from the special forces of Charles Taylor's National Patriotic Front of Liberia (NPFL), intervened in Sierra Leone in an attempt to overthrow the Joseph Momoh's government. The resulting civil war which lasted nearly 11 years enveloped the country. Alluvial Diamonds helped to arm the RUF. To maintain control of important mining districts like Kono, thousands of civilians were expelled and kept away. Gold mining equally fueled the war.

Child soldiers were recruited and coerced at the barrel of a gun to join the ranks of the Revoluntary United Front (RUF). A grassroots militia force- "THE KAMAJORS" operated to defend family and home due to the Sierra Leone Army (SLA) perceived incompetenc. On 18 January 2002, President Kabbah declared the eleven year Sierra Leone war officially over. By most estimates over 50, 000 people had lost their lives during the war. Tens of thousands fled to neighboring countries. A large proportion of the refugees fled abroad.

MALI WAR

Since 16 January 2012, several insurgent groups have been waging a campaign against the Malian government for the independence or greater autonomy for an area in Northern Mali known as AZAWAD. Under the leadership of Bilal Ag Acherif, the National Movement for the liberation of Azawad (MNLA), an organization fighting to make Azawad an independent homeland for the Tuareg people, had taken control of the region by April, 2012.

On 22 March, 2012 President Amadou Toumani Toure was ousted in a coup d 'etat over the handling of the crisis, a month before a presidential election was to have taken place. Mutinous soldiers, calling themselves the National Committee for the Restoration of Democracy and State (CNRDR) took control and suspended the constitution of Mali. There was instability in the country as fighting ensued. FRENCH, ECOWAS and UN troops were deployed to Mali. Tens of thousands of refugees emerged during the war. Many of the refugees are now living in France.

APARTHEID REGIME IN SOUTH AFRICA

Though Nelson Rolihlahla Mandela was the arrowhead of anti-apartheid movement, other anti-apartheid activists were Oliver Reginald Kaizana Tambo, Walter Max Ulyate Sisulu, Steve Biko, Desmond Tutu, Helen Suzman and Denis Brutus. With the enactment of apartheid laws in 1948, racial discrimination was institutionalized. Race laws touched every aspects of social life, including a prohibition of marriage between non-whites and whites and the sanctioning of "WHITE ONLY" jobs.

All South Africans were racially classified into three categories WHITE, BLACK (African) and COLORED (of mixed decent). Non compliance with the race laws were dealt with harshly. Africans living in the homelands needed passport to enter South Africa. They were aliens in their country. In 1960, a large group of black Africans in Sharpeville refused to carry passes which made the government to declare a state of emergency.

The emergency lasted for 156 days, leaving 69 people dead and 187 people wounded because of unjust laws of apartheid. Indiscriminate shooting of black Africans in the city of Soweto was a regular occurrence. Thousands of people died in custody after gruesome acts of torture.

Those who were very unlucky were tried, sentenced to death, banished, or imprisoned for life like Nelson Mandela. Oliver Tambo and multitude of South Africans fled into exile. Precisely, Oliver Tambo fled to the United Kingdom where he lived from 1960 to 1990 in Alexandra Park Road (Muswell Hill) in the London Borough of Haringey. In this abode, he led a campaign for the imposition of sanctions (economic, sports, e.t.c.) against the evil regime of Apartheid in South Africa.

HIV/AIDS DISEASE

Since its discovery in 1981, HIV/AIDS has killed millions of Africans. The African continent is probably most affected by HIV and AIDS, with Sub-Saharan Africa being the worst affected region. In short 70% of the world's Aids cases are in the continent of Africa. Botswana is the worst affected country. At a time 33.8 % of people of Botswana between the ages of 15 and 49 carry the deadly disease. Out of 10 AIDS affected countries in the world 9 are in Africa. South Africa is the country in the world, (not only among African countries) with most HIV/AIDS patients.

Mandela in Xhosa clothing in 1962, the year he was convicted of sabotage

The ANC leader, Mandela, arrives at his treason trial in 1958. He was then sent to Robben Island

Nelson Mandela inside the jail at Robben Island where he served 27 years with Walter Sisulu, a leading light in the African National Congress.

The 2007 UNAIDS report estimated that 5,700,000 South Africans have HIV/AIDS. That is about 12% of South African population of 48 million. Swaziland was believed to have the world's highest rate of HIV infection with almost four of 10 adults infected with HIV. Life expectancy, healthcare, Schools and economic growth have been affected. Tens of thousands have fled the continent for fear of contracting the deadly disease.

DESERTIFICATION

Desertification is a type of land degradation in which a relatively dry land becomes increasingly arid, typically losing its bodies of water as well as vegetation and wildlife. It is caused by a variety of factors, such as climate change and the removal of vegetation. Desertification is a significant ecological and environmental problem in most part of Africa.

Most Fertile lands in Africa are speedily transforming into arid desert, typically as a result of deforestation, drought or improper agriculture. Desertification has caused the displacement of local populations. The Sahara is currently expanding South at a rate of up to 48 Kilometers per year.

Business Entrepreneurs are avers to invest in arid zones. This absence of investment contributes to marginalisation of these zones. Desertification often causes lands to become unable to support the same sized population that previously lived there. Desertification of soils appears to be one of the fundamental causes of hunger in Africa. This results in mass migrations out of the zones into other parts of Africa or the Diaspora. As kofi Annan the former Secretary-General of United Nation said in 2006, "if we don't take action, current trends suggest that by 2020 an estimated 60 million Sub-Saharan Africans could move toward North Africa and Europe due to desertification".

FAMINE

Oxford dictionary of English, third edition, defines famine as extreme and general scarcity of food in a town, country, etc. According to the British Broadcasting Corporation (BBC) of Monday 11 November, 2002, AFRICA'S FAMINE: Country by Country, the BBC reporter declared that the following

African countries have at one time or the other suffered from famine. They are Ethiopia, Eritrea, Mauritania, Angola, Zambia, Mozambique, Malawi, Lesotho and Swaziland.

In 1984 Ethiopia suffered severe famine. In 2012 the situation reached crisis level. The prolonged drought which brought hunger to Ethiopia also hit its northern neighbor of Eritrea. When it occurred in Zambia, the government declared the country's food shortage a national disaster. In Angola, medical relief organization, Medecins Sans Frontiers (MSF) estimates that at least 1.5 million people suffered from acute malnutrition.

There was severe dry spells and drought in 2001/2002 season in Northern Mozambique. In Malawi, President Bakili Muluzi declared a state of Emergency as Maize production fell by 40%. The 2005/2006 Niger food crisis was very severe.

It affected the regions of Northern Maradi, Tahoua, Tillaberi and Zinder. In the affected areas, 2.4 million of 3.6 million people were considered highly vulnerable to food insecurity. By extension the Famine also affected Chad and Northern Burkina Faso.

In July 2012, the United Nations warned that hundreds of millions of pounds are needed to prevent another scourge of Famine in Somalia. Thousands of Somalis have been fleeing the Country each week in search of food and water. Nearly half a million children are at risk of dying from malnutrition and disease.

FLOOD DISASTER ACROSS AFRICA

Flood disaster has been a recurring nightmare across Africa. Devastating rainstorm often characterise the weather condition across Africa. Flooding have destroyed lives and property across the continent. The construction of the Aswan Dam in the 1960's stopped the yearly inundation and annual flood of the Nile.

Ogunpa disaster in Nigeria of 1980 gave"OGUNPA" national and international notoriety. After about 12 hours of heavy downpour, Ibadan was virtually left in ruins. Hundreds of bodies were retrieved from the debris of collapsed houses, and vehicles were washed away by the deluge. The flood killed hundreds of people and destroyed property of a whole generation of residents. To memorize the "OMIYALE TRAGEDY", many songs were rendered by leading Juju artistes. Many displaced Ibadan residents left the shores of Nigeria.

BBC News of February 11, 2000 reported that freak floods hit South Africa and Mozambique and claimed scores of lives and left more than 100,000 people homeless. Human bodies and cattle carcasses floated on the water. People resorted to drinking filthy flood water.

In 2001 in Algeria, hundreds of people died from floods while violent storm killed hundreds of people. In 2007, Volta River burst its banks. A lot of damages were left in its trail. In August 2007 the Sudanese government and the UN launched an appeal to raise 20 million dollars to help more than 400,000 people hit by floods across Sudan. Sudanese officials described the floods as the worst in living memory. There were reported cases of cholera outbreak orchestrated by the flood.

In September 2007 flood misery hit Africa. An estimated one million people across Africa were hit by rains which had destroyed crops, burst dams and left thousands dead. In September 2009 Burkina Faso, Senegal, Ghana and Niger were hit by flood. 600,000 people were affected. In August 2010, flood displaced more than 2 million people in Nigeria after flood gates on two Dams were opened to release rising waters along the Niger River.

In January 2011, heavy flooding left at least 50 people dead in Johannesburg, South Africa (Source CNN). Dozens were killed as homes and buildings collapsed around them. Flood washed away bridges and destroyed roads. In the same 2011, 23 people died in Tanzania as a result of flooding while 4,000 people were displaced, state run media reported. Three consecutive days of rain, the heaviest in 57 years, caused the flooding.

Again in the City of Ibadan, BBC Africa of August 28, 2011 reported that at least 20 people were killed and thousands were displaced by flooding.

At least 11 people have died after sudden rains caused flooding in Mauritanian Capital of PORT LOUIS in March, 2013. Millions of citizens, scared of recurring flooding had fled the continent.

EDUCATIONAL PURSUIT ABROAD

In over six decades, millions of African youths have left the shores of the continent to study abroad. There are so many reasons why these Millions of frustrated youths bolted out of the continent to fulfill their educational dreams. These are the push factors responsible for the exodus of Africans to study overseas:

Most schools in Africa are ill-equipped and poorly funded. Many courses of study are not available on demand. Most of the Universities and Polytechnics are glorified secondary schools. On completion of study, the graduates are placed on very poor salary structure. Television channels are not helping matters: they show better quality of life in foreign destinations. Apart from her youths suffering racial attack abroad, Africa's brain drain is the host countries' brain gain.

PLAYING PROFESSIONAL SPORTS ABROAD

Another push factor is the urge by African sports men and women to travel overseas to participate in professional sports. For the past five decades, talented sports men and women have been leaving the continent of Africa to sign for professional sports abroad.

Attractive pay coupled with very good standard of living abroad had forced many youths to abandon the Africas' sports federations. They hire agents to negotiate contract deals. They sign for variety of sports such as: Football, Handball, Boxing, Basket-ball, Rugby, Hockey, Table tennis, Badminton, Lawn tennis, Swimming, Wrestling, etc. While plying their trades in the diaspora, many are subjected to all manners of racial attacks.

MARITAL TIES, FAMILY RE-UNION AND ADOPTIONS

Finally, Africans emigrate to effect marital ties, family re-union and adoption. Wives and husbands who are married to Africans living abroad travel abroad to join up with their spouses. Also wards and children born to Africans living abroad arrange visas to join up with their parents. Adoption of African children by foreigners has been going on for decades. The adopted children had to leave the shores of Africa to join up with their adopted parents abroad.

Income from even the most menial jobs in Europe is in stark contrast to the lucrative employment in crushing poverty environments of such nations as Senegal, Guinea or Eritrea. And it appears that the disparity can only be widened by the growing population and desertification of sub-Saharan Africa. Instability across much of the continent, notably in the Horn of Africa, is also fuelling mass migration.

There is hunger and starvation across the continent. When many Africans have breakfast, there is no money for lunch or dinner. Lately many poor African immigrants now realise that the southern border of Spain and northern fringe of Africa is the shortest distance between Europe and the African continent. But it is a most shameful abyss that separates us. With very bad governments to contend with across Africa, coupled with abject poverty, many poor people are forced to leave for greener pastures abroad.

To worsen the situation, a few rich people flaunt their ill-gotten wealth in the midst of squalor and poverty. Bad roads, poor housing, epileptic power supply, lack of adequate food supply, insecurity of life and property, communal dispute, land disputes, cynicism, internecine war, civil war, disease, drought and famine are some of the reasons that finally push people to relocate abroad.

Cheap international travel, 24 hours media that spread words of opportunity everywhere are all multiplying the choices for those looking to improve their lot: Africans currently track events in Europe and America on satellite television.

Because of the unprecedented influx of African immigrants, European Union governments and commissions have recently been studying how Mauritania can be helped to deal with migration between its northern coast and the Spanish territory of the Canary Islands. Around 1000 sub-Saharan Africans arrive in the Mauritanian port of Nouadhibou each month, wanting to be smuggled into Europe, often in unsafe fishing vessels.

Migration from Mauritania has increased since Morocco, previously one of the main transit points for Africans hoping to enter Europe, tightened its border controls in 2007. The Mauritanian government had proposed to do a lot about it, but it has to deal with border controls, provisions of camps for immigrations and sending back migrants expelled from Europe to their home countries.

Here in Europe, asylum seekers bound for the European Union, frequently have to undertake perilous journeys. Deaths caused by drowning or suffocation during transit illustrate how voyages of hope can sometimes become voyages of disaster.

The maximum permitted lengths of detention vary from 72 hours in Denmark to an indefinite period of time in the UK and the Netherlands. Germany, Malta and Latvia allow detention for 18 months or longer. They fail to realise that 6 months as a maximum duration of detention is too long for an administrative measure. In general, the rules on immigration detention in European Union states are very vague. The criteria are less clear about who can be detained, why an imigrant is detained and for how long.

African migrants may have already suffered imprisonment and torture in the country from which they fled. The consequences of detention amount to "inhuman and degrading treatment". And still the Africans keep coming.

On September 6, 2006, "The Voice" newspaper on page 10 reported that 80 bodies had been retrieved after an immigrant boat capsized off the coast of Mauritania on its way to the Canaries. Such incidents have little deterrent effect for Africans on passage to fortress Europe, America and Asia. Thousands of dehydrated and dying Africans arrive at the Canary Islands on wooden boats.

This chapter remains inconclusive without mentioning the activities of people smugglers or human traffickers. They lure young unsuspecting girls and boys out of their homes with the promise of getting them a good job on reaching abroad.

The smugglers often achieve this with the aid and connivance of the poor or greedy parents or guardians of the children being trafficked. Teenagers as young as 11, 12, 13 and 14 years of age are urged to go abroad to "make it". They lose their childhood, they become disoriented and feel dislocated from all people. They are sold like cargo and often forced to serve as sexual objects to all manners of people. Some of them are gang raped and most are sexually exploited.

If these young and innocent girls and boys were white children, a severe and harsh law would long have been promulgated against the traffickers. This is another case of racism, this time, against African minors.

CHAPTER FOUR

My Encounter with Racism

I was deeply enmeshed in the politics of my local community of Owa now Evbuobanosa way back in the mid '80s which nearly culminated in my being elected as the councilor of my ward. On May 1, 1989 at the verge of completing my bachelor's degree from the University of Nigeria, Nsukka, I wrote a critique against the military junta of Nigeria.

The critique which was published in the Nigeria Observer of May 1, 1989, entitled "**NO TEARS FOR POLITICIANS**" was too abusive of the military establishment that I feared persecution and a definite prosecution if I was arrested. I was informed by friends that plain clothes State Security Service [SSS] operatives could be wanting to track me down. I was seriously advised to be on the look out. When I realised that my life was no longer safe and secured, I had to plan my exit from Nigeria. Upon completion of my final degree examinations at the University of Nigeria, Nsukka, I hurriedly arranged my departure from the shores of my beloved country, Nigeria.

I fixed Poland Visa on my passport and headed to Balkan Airline for my flight ticket. Balkan Airline is the flagship national airline of

Gen. Sani Abacha
Nigeria Military Ruler (1993-1998)

Bulgaria. It was the Airline that flew me in June, 1990 to Warsaw Poland. We took off from Lagos in Nigeria and landed for some hours stopover in Sophia the capital city of Bulgaria. We all deplaned and headed towards the lounge to relax for the final leg journey from Sofia to Warsaw.

To my consternation, as soon as we took off from Sofia cigarette smoke was billowing out from the cockpit. Definitely, either the pilot or the co-pilot was smoking cigarette. When I looked around almost all the passengers that joined us for the last leg of the flight from Sofia to Warsaw were smoking one type of cigarette or the other. I saw that cigarette ashtrays were fixed to the part of the seat where passengers rest their hands. I was surprised. As they smoked, they stubbed the cigarettes' ends in the Ash-trays. Co-African passengers were confused as to who to complain to. We grew annoyed and were shouting at them to stop smoking.

At a point, one of the air hostesses told us that if we can not bear the smoke we should switch on the air ventilator above our heads to absorb the smoke. As we were fast approaching Chopin international airport in Warsaw, I observed that most of the passengers that had complained against smoking on the aircraft were now been more concerned with how to scale through the checks of the Polish immigration and Custom services.

They kept smoking until we successfully landed in the freezy and breezy weather of Warsaw. After a successful custom and immigration clearance into Poland, I planned my next move into continental Europe. Poland was practicing communism and the wind of change was slowly but gradually blowing across communist countries all over the world. I felt that Poland could not be my final destination. Germany, or West Germany as it was named then, was the most attractive destination.

Poland was extremely cold even in the month of June when I arrived there. The weather was very inhospitable. It was windy all the time; chilly, freezy and wet. In 1989 the notoriously famous Berlin Wall had just been brought down. The huge socio-political, economic and psychological barrier separating East and West Germany were down with it. We were five Nigerians who had to pay and negotiate with people smugglers that operated between Poland and Germany. We eventually paid our way through. The passage between Poland and Germany was a harrowing experience. I gnashed my teeth as we approached Goethe border post between Poland and East Germany. We set out to cross the border in the thick of the night to avoid being caught.

On approaching the immigration checking point, our smuggler, who was already known to the custom and immigration officer, had no hard time convincing the officers at Goethe that we were going to Germany for a short visit, and that we were not going to overstay our visas to Poland. God forbid if we were refused entry, it would mean we can never set foot on German soil. I held my breath.

It was a heart stopping experience. Our passports were collected from us and handed over to immigration officers. After about 10 minutes, our smugglers came back and told us that we have been allowed to enter East Germany. After traveling the whole night through East Germany, we eventually crossed into West Germany without any further border checks and controls. It took about 5 hours to travel between Goethe border post and West Berlin.

When we arrived about 6am, I was relieved and we all hugged ourselves and jubilated. We asked for the address and direction of where we could seek political asylum. We were directed to Tegel, a suburb of Berlin. When we reached Tegel, we surrendered ourselves as political asylum seekers. We were interviewed and housed in a makeshift hostel vacated by the US Air force based in Tegel.

I spent 4 months in Tegel with the other refugees from Africa and the former Yugoslavia until we were dispersed and posted to other parts of Germany. I was posted to Munich, the capital city of the state of Bayern, the home of BMW Motors fabrics. As political asylum seekers, we were not allowed to travel outside Munich. Our rights to freedom of movement were curtailed.

MY EXPERIENCE OF RACISM IN GERMANY

Those days, consciously or not, ordinary citizens and government bureaucrats still clung to the notion that Germany was a unique homogenous people. There was a conspicuous lack of public debate in Germany those days about how an insular country like Germany should adjust to the reality that more African migrants are coming and that those already there are changing Germany. Racism was palpable. It was very, very rampant and thick in the air. You could feel it.

You could even smell it. Redskins members with shaven heads dotted the nooks and crannies of Germany. They were identified with their trademark chants of "AuslanderRaus" -meaning foreigners leave. Redskin heads wore swastikas, wielded knives, cutlasses and broken bottles. Acid attacks were rampant. They poured acid on foreigners, particularly Africans. The attacks perpetrated against Africans were at its peak during the anniversary of the notorious 'Christal night'.

The Neo-Nazis as they were rebranded took over the streets. The 'Christal night' was the night Adolf Hitler declared total war of annihilation against the Jews in Munich. The Neo-Nazis keep the tradition and in celebrating the anniversary vent their anger against Africans who they now feel have replaced the Jews.

The German government "Bundesregerung" barred asylum seekers from working. To compound the problems, there was incessant financial demands from home. I broke the rule as I had to work. I was caught 10 times, locked up for up to 12 hours on each occasion.

In Germany, we were housed in conditions that offended human dignity. We were loaded into containers, cramped together, almost suffocating to death. During the summers, the thick steel of the container was ionised during the heat of the day so much that it almost seized oxygen within the container. In winter it was extremely cold inside the containers. There is extreme temperature reversal. Winter was extremely cold inside the containers.

The metal steel inversely retained a lot of cold and the retention translated to extreme cold temperature. We often joked and teased ourselves that the wicked immigration officers could lock up the container one of those nights and ship us to anywhere in Africa.

Fights often broke out among the occupants of the containers-orchestrated by poor living conditions and concomitant frustration. It was a hopeless situation. On the streets of Munich my encounter with brazen display of racism was suffocating.

The Germans would only give a bit of respect to black Americans and not to black Africans. Immediately they come at you, they would want to size you up to know whether you are an African or an American. So on discovering this bias, prejudice and hatred towards black Africans, we had to adapt our ways of life to suit their taste.

So all we did was to be as much as possible like the black Americans. If you appeared unkempt, you were less regarded and tagged an African who was never wanted in any place. Our mode of dress had to closely resemble that of the Yankees. We had to change our tropical voices to rhyme with the American slang. 'Polizei', the name of the German police whose uniform resembles our defunct Nigeria airways, were notoriously ubiquitous in excessively policing black Africans. After 2 years of waiting on my decision, and being treated like glorified prisoner, I became weary and snappy in character. One night, one of the co-occupants of the container confronted me for no reason. Fighting ensued between me and him. The fight was reported to the authorities. The aftermath of the fracas triggered a forced and accelerated hearing of my case. In short, forces were against me.

My asylum request was brought to an abrupt end. My application was callously rejected without due process. Fearing a possible arrest on returning back to Nigeria, I planned with a friend who connected me to one Edokpolor- a people smuggler based in Basel in Switzerland. In the thick of the night, he drove a Mercedes Benz car and we traveled into the city of Basel in Switzerland. On reaching the border post between Germany and Switzerland, he hid me in the boot of his car and sped past the immigration post.

Luckily for us there were no immigration and custom personnel at the border post. If I had been caught I would have been handed over to the German immigration officers who would definitely and hurriedly deport me to Nigeria. I was rehabilitated in Basel for 2 weeks before I was handed over to another handler who ferried me to Zurich. In Zurich I applied for political asylum. As an asylum seeker, we had a limited right to do only menial jobs.

MY EXPERIENCES OF RACISM IN SWITZERLAND

The path to becoming Swiss is one paved with prejudice and racism. If you are an African, you face an uphill struggle to call the Alpine nation home. Being born in Switzerland does not mean Swiss citizenship.

A person must have lived in the country legally for at least 12 years. He or she then go before a commune committee to answer questions, ranging from the neutral ("do you speak German") to the more controversial ("can you imagine marrying a Swiss boy?"). Meaning can you practise homosexuality? Then the commune, that is the local authority, voted in secret to accept or reject. Decisions arrived at by "direct democracy" can end up being arbitrary or racially motivated.

When I was in Zurich in Switzerland, I attended "Grace International Christian Church in Oerlikon". The congregation was split into cell groups for the purpose of house fellowship. I was grouped with Dr Michael Steven a Singaporean who lectures at the University of Zurich main campus, located on Ramistrasse 71, CH-8006 Zurich. We conducted our house fellowship every midweek (Wednesday) evening in Dr Michael Steven's house. After Prayer, Praise and worship and studying the Bible we normally break for refreshment.

During the break, Dr Michael serves us bread and tea. We Africans eventually observed that Dr Michael always served hard bread only to Africans while he served soft bread to his fellow white Christians. It got to a point and I asked Dr Michael why the discriminatory service. I queried why I was served very hard bread and not soft one. He and his wife laughed off the question. That means that all along it was intentionally done.

One Friday evening, I strolled into a pub as I was a bit lonely and wanted to spice my evening with good music and drinks. I entered one famous local pub very close to Parade Place -but the Swiss call it Pa-ra-de Platz. When I sat down I ordered a drink, the barman winced and refused to ac-knowledge my presence and what I had ordered. When I stated that I had been ignored, he passed a racist comment and went further to call me names, he even told me to go back to Africa.

I replied to the racist taunt. I told him that the money that fuels the economy of Switzerland and provides employment for the people comes principally from stolen and laundered money from corrupt military and civilian rulers from Nigeria. He answered "and so what?" he said "you black monkeys should steal more and bring them here for us to enjoy". I was infuriated and told him I will deal with him. I was still boiling over his racist remarks when he pushed me out and shut the door against my face.

After some minutes, I tiptoed to the place and hurled very heavy stones at the glass door everything came crashing down and immediately I fled the scene. I took corners and bends to avoid being traced or chased by anyone. Unluckily, I was apprehended by the police. My heart was racing- what came to my mind was the fear of forced deportation back to Nigeria.

But I was very surprised by the outcome of the arrest and interrogation by the police because they returned a not guilty verdict on me. I was flabbergasted to learn that the police were in fact in total support of me, they told me that racism was getting too much against Africans and there was an anti-racism campaign going on now in government circles. I was let off the hook.

Unfortunately after getting freed trouble came knocking from another direction. My application for political refugee status was turned down by the Swiss authorities and my lawyer on receiving the negative decision from the Ministry of Justice, Immigration and Naturalisation Department, had deliberately held my letters and refused to send the decision.

The racist lawyer willfully held the letter from Bern the Swiss capital. The implication was that after 4 weeks I could not apply for an appeal of the rejection before the mandatory 4 weeks of appeal expired. Very early one morning an immigration plain clothed police officer forcefully knocked on my door. The diminutive man shouted and flexed his arms at me. He queried why I am still in Switzerland. I asked him what he meant.

They had played another bad one against me. This was a devilish conspiracy visited on me. He queried that my asylum request was rejected more than a month ago and I failed to appeal within the stipulated four (4) week period. I answered back that I had not been communicated and as a result I could not appeal. I have never been informed of any rejection, I said.

He demanded my temporary asylum seekers identity card from me and I obliged. After snatching it from my hand, he thrusted a prepared and pre-signed note into my palm instructing me to go to my embassy in Bern to obtain my Traveling Certificate (TC).

At this time the military junta in Nigeria led by General Ibrahim Babangida had just left government for Ernest Shokekan who was in turn toppled by General Sani Abacha. I surreptitiously returned to Munich thinking that I would not face any further problems having stayed away for about a year.

I traveled down hopeful to revive my asylum request. On returning back to Germany, I was arrested by the foreign police and a deportation order was quickly sought and obtained from the court. They told me that the foreign police had been looking for me for deportation. I was locked up in Munich prison for three months after which I was flown back to Nigeria via Sheremetyevo international airport in Moscow.

On arriving Moscow Sheremetyevo International Airport, we transit passengers were deplaned and taken to the terminal building by apron buses. At the airport I had to wait for any Aeroflot aircraft flying to Nigeria.

At this time, the Russian economy was worse than many African country's economies. For four days, while I was awaiting an onward flight to Nigeria, I was fed on watery pepper soup with very, very hard bread. On two occasions I attempted to sneak past Moscow immigration. But I was caught and hurriedly flown to Lagos. Throughout the journey to Nigeria, I felt I was just like a piece of cargo. I was distraught. I felt worthless. On touching down, I vowed to stage a come back.

After a shortwhile, I was able to wangle my way back to Europe. This time I went in through Amsterdam. At SCHIPOL INTERNATIONAL AIRPORT in Amsterdam, I was handed a letter instructing me to go and register as a political asylum seeker in a little village called Riyksbergen. Riyksbergen is a small Dutch community in the south of the country.

After some days there, I was posted to a refugee holding center in a village called Heyen. Heyen is another small Dutch town in the region of Brabant, whose headquarters is Maastricht. While there, I joined the Nigerian political pressure group called "Nigeria Democratic Movement" (NDM). I eventually rose through the rank and file to become the National Secretary General of the association.

MY RACISM EXPERIENCES AND THE POLITICAL STRUGGLES IN THE NETHERLANDS

In the heat of my activism while in the Netherlands, I wrote against the regime of General Sani Abacha which was published in the Newsweek magazine of August 26, 1996.

I openly abused and denounced the government of the late maximum dictator of Nigeria, General Sani Abacha. Newsweek magazine has a worldwide audience and certainly the General's helmsmen were more concerned and sensitive about outside opinion against the military government. *Newsweek* magazine was then the flagship of world news magazines. Certainly my critique got the attention of Abacha and his henchmen in Nigeria and abroad.

The immigration authority in the Netherlands were well aware of the risk implication of sending me back to Nigeria while General Sani Abacha held sway. The Dutch immigration authority - "Immigratie and Naturalisatie Dienst"- were adamant to my plea and my political asylum request was turned down. Even when there was an international outcry against the maximum dictator General Sani Abacha to relinquish power, Shell BP - a consortium of Shell Holland and British petroleum were too busy producing oil for the General and his ill fated government.

The Netherlands authority feigned opposition to the dictator but deep down they did a lot of economic dealings with him. I was harangued and harassed out of the refugee camp at Heyen by the immigration police. I had to flee to a neighbouring country, Belgium, where I vowed never to seek political asylum again.

I lived in Belgium illegally until there was a proclamation of general amnesty to all illegal immigrants by an act of Parliament in October 1999. It came into force in January 2000. I cashed into the golden opportunity and filed application papers for the regularisation of my stay. In September 2001 my residency permit was regularised. Since the Belgian and Nigerian governments lay claim to dual citizenship, I applied to be a citizen of Belgium which was granted.

RACISM IN BELGIUM - MY EXPERIENCES

In April 2004, I got a job to work in a pigment producing factory in a small community call Bornem, which is about 10 kilometers from Antwerp, the second largest city in Belgium. When I started the job, little did I know that the so called pigments (colour paint) we produce were laced with very lethal and toxic chemical components. I worked in this company for one year and I fell ill. Before I knew it, I had contracted a disease. I contacted my family doctor, Dr (Mrs) Jacobs, my house doctor in Antwerp, who sent me to a clinic for blood screening.

After the blood test, six harmful chemicals were found in my blood in dangerous and harmful quantities. After the astonishing discovery, she advised me to apply to a compensation fund. I applied to the fund but they replied that my disease could not be classified as a professional sickness just because I was an African.

As long as I am not sick of malaria fever and with the dangerous quantities of chemicals still found in my blood, their statement is not short of racism and marginalisation against another black African. They know that fundamentally speaking, there is a clear difference between a natural and a professional disease.

If I were a white Belgian, I could have been compensated to the tune of about 1 million euros. I was misused by the company and dumped by the authority that is responsible to compensate me for the disease I contracted while at work.

CHAPTER FIVE

Racial Conflicts and Problems of Acculturation and Enculturation

Rodney Glen King, born in Sacramento in California was the symbol of police racism. It was the night of March 3, 1991 when Police spotted a white Hyundai speeding. King at the wheels was pursued by oficers on a high-speed chase. When the pursuit eventually ended King was ordered to lie face down on a concrete and asphalted road. The officers swarmed on him. He was given an electric Taser shock then hit with more than 50 baton strokes.

He was savagely beaten to what he later said was "an inch from death". As they beat him, King said the officers yelled, **"WE ARE GOING TO KILL YOU NIGGER"**. The attack left King with several injuries including a fractured skull, a damage to internal organs, his face bruised and swollen, his right eye

The face that shamed a nation: Rodney King, three days after his beatinig. A year later, four police officers charged over the affair walked free from court, promoting riots in Los Angeles which had to be quelled by the National Guard.

reduced to a bloody pulp, all of which were captured on video by a nearby resident George Holliday, who came out on to his balcony after woken by sirens. As dawn broke he was operated on for five hours.

Holliday latter passed the footage on to a local TV network from which it was soon taken up by US media across the country. However in April 29, 1992 a jury with no black members acquitted three of the officers and a mistrial was declared for the fourth. Violence erupted immediately starting in south Los Angeles.

Police were outnumbered and the riot spread to the City's Korea town area. The riots lasted for several days and left 55 people dead, more than 2000 injured and large part of Los Angeles on fire as authorities struggled to contain the violence. A damage estimated at 1 billion dollars was caused to property.

"I have respect for the police. Some of them tried to make it up to me"

It is almost certain that there would have been no consequences for the police involved had not an unseen witness, George Holliday been keen to test out his new video camera. Widespread racism in the largely white male force was exposed. Around the 20th anniversary of the riots in April of 2012, before his untimely death in his house garden swimming pool, Rodney King gave a series of interviews saying that racism still needed to be challenged.

Asia and Europe do not have civil rights movements to address the mighty challenge of integrating its African immigrants. The problems of Acculturation and Enculturation (integration) is more pronounced in Europe and Asia because of the absence of civil rights movements. Although Asian and European immigrants some said, were not like African-Americans-they chose to come to Europe and Asia. Others stressed that European and Asian immigrants are not legally segregated as African-Americans were. A more practical objection was that Europe and Asia immigrant communities are not unified or organised enough to create such a movement. There is some truth to these arguments, but they miss the broader purpose of the analogy.

There is little doubt, to begin with, that in Europe and Asia African immigrants are visible minorities, who are marginalized as were African-Americans. Their chances of success in schools and employment lag markedly behind those of natives. In terms of representation, African immigrants are woefully absent from politics and public institutions. France's urban riots in the autumn of 2005 recalled the demonstrations in America in the 1950's and 1960's.

But my primary reason for invoking the civil rights movement is to understand how miserly is Europe's commitment to immigrant integration today. Even the continent's progressive politicians cannot consistently find the courage to advocate the merits of immigration and equal opportunities. Instead, they are far more likely to jump on the bandwagon of cracking down on illegal immigration. Compare that with how the then United States of America Attorney General, Robert Kennedy would furiously order George Wallace to defend the right of young black Africans to attend Alabama schools.

Commitment to affirmative action had leveled the playing field occasioned by aggressive anti-discrimination judicial action. There is no comparable effort being made in Europe, despite a problem of equal or even greater magnitude and arguably of worse potential consequences.

Take this statement by President George. W. Bush shortly after the September 11 terrorist attacks, as reported in the Financial Times of September 20th, 2001 he said ; "America treasures the relationship with its many Muslim friends and it respects the vibrant faith of Islam which inspires countless individuals to lead lives of honesty, integrity and morality". At moments of crisis, by contrast, European leaders have resorted to a " we won't take this anymore "adversarial rhetoric that polarises the public, or to implementing integration tests that can frankly be outright offensive.

African immigrants awaiting deportation are often held in administrative detention for as long as 18 months. In a number of EU countries, there is no upper limit on detention length. And they have spread outside of Europe to places like Libya. It has become more worrisome in a situation where Italy builds and pays for detention centers to house Africans it plans to deport. Even the best centers are strung with cameras and coils of barbed wire, while the worst detention centers are infested with vermin and lack medical care.The psychological impact of incarceration can be severe, particularly for the young.

The Netherlands in the year 2008 has planned to shift some of its detainees to two floating platforms. In Ireland and Germany, detention centres are usually in prisons. Many others are in airports like those in Vienna, Paris, Lisbon, Amsterdam,

Manchester and London. Many smaller holding centres, containing 20 people or less, are dotted around Europe and America with little outside observation on conditions in the camps which often fall far below international norms.

Refugees are condemned to destitution and most refugees sleep in rough apartments. Residents of Samos in Greece are still reeling from the exposure of conditions in their old detention centre, a former tobacco factory where arrivals were assailed by stench of vomit, urine and sweat. Where sewage seeped into the dormitories and severe overcrowding meant people slept in rows on the floor.

The average length of detention in camps around Europe is 12 to 18 months. In France it is 32 days, in Spain 40 days, Italy 60 days and in Greece 3 months. Germany has no upper limit for asylum seekers, while a visit to Malta by members of the European Parliament in March, 2006 found that some Africans had been in detention for more than 5 years. Many Africans are squatting in makeshift tents surrounded by their few belongings and surviving on water. Interpreters, medical doctors and legal aids are often not on hand for those needing to request protection. Most centres fail to uphold rights to family, rights to minors and the right to physical integrity or protection given the psychological effects of long periods of incarceration.

They just think these Africans are numbers surviving on water and salt alone. Many Africans go on hunger strike- they look sick, discoloured, frail and weak and with some of them already having been in and out of hospital on more than one occasion. Even those that have residency permits are no longer exempt.

Most African men and their children are becoming involved in gang cultures. They do so because they feel they have no choice and no future. As a society, they are failing young black kids. In recent years the inner London district has been the scene of a series of horrific street crimes including the murder of schoolboy Damilola Taylor in 2000.

A story was carried on Monday October 29th, 2007 in the UK Independent newspaper that an African engineer who traveled to Northern Ireland for a holiday was dubiously detained because he was black. Frank Kakopa of Zimbabwe spent two days in the high security Maghaberry Prison in Co. Antrim in Northern Ireland despite having produced papers from his employer confirming that he was living and working in the UK. He was also strip-searched. Mr Kakopa, a structural engineer, was working in Liverpool and Warrington when he took his wife and children aged 6 and 12 to Northern Ireland for a few days in August 2005. He was locked up with convicted criminals having committed no crime. Mr Kakopa believed he was detained simply because he was a black African.

Being a black African makes you ultra visible to the extent that the shop assistant will follow you around the shop as soon as you enter. Yet the presence of black Africans in Europe and America goes back centuries. The flipside of the coin is the disproportionate visibility accorded to black people when the media reports on crime resulting in the sort of fear that makes white people cross the road the minute a young black man comes into view. Where negative stereotypes are concerned, we Africans remain the most visible of the ethnic minorities.

CHAPTER SIX

Racial Discrimination as it Affects Africans in the Diaspora

Immigration is the biggest concern for most people in developed countries, and they want the law toughened up. They feel the laws on immigration should be much tougher. They often complain that their biggest concern is pressure on public services and jobs. Geography pits the European Union on the defensive against the inflow as thousands of migrants try to pierce EU borders. The well targeted Lampedusa, off Italy and the Canary Islands, the Spanish territory off West Africa are locations where refugees try to land after traveling hundreds of kilometers in delapidated boats.

From a continent of rich ancient civilisation, Africa degenerated to its citizens exporting continent. Europe and America claim they are buckling under the strain. They are broadly not sympathetic to the migrants. But when European powers partitioned Africa and Africans in 1884/1885 in Berlin, there was no conference. Africa was partitioned, occupied, possessed and exploited by the Europeans and the Americans.

On May 11, 2006 Hans Van Themsche in Antwerp, Belgium, shaved his head, took a bus to collect money from his account and returned to buy a hunting rifle. In his rampage through the streets, he killed Mali born nanny, Outematou Niangadou and toddler, Luna Drowart. He decided to shoot because Outematou was an African.

It is widely believed that the Vlaams Belang, the extreme right anti immigration party is partly morally responsible for the tragedy. Vlaams Belang has a great deal of support in Antwerp and Van Themsche's aunt is one of its MP's.

Bini born Mr Aikpitanyi was killed by immigration officers in Spain. They claimed that he resisted deportation to Nigeria and this is the reason why they snufed the life out of him.

In Florence, Africans at home and abroad mourned after a gunman Killed two Senegalese street vendors and injured several others on Tuesday the 13th of December, 2011 in the Italian City of Florence. Gunman Gianuca Casseri, 50 has been linked to a far right group. Gianuca Casseri an Italian with fascist sympathies has links to a Far right anti- immigration movement called Cassa Pound, founded in 2003, which has about 5,000 members and draws inspiration from the fascist regime of Benito Mussolini. Gianuca Casseri lived on his own in Tuscan country side.

Gianuca Casseri

He was a member of the right wing community group. He was resident at Cireglio in the Province of Pistoia but also had a home in Florence. He drove into Dalmazia in his white Golf Volkswagen car. He parked at a newsstand near some traffic lights and then walked to the small market where Senegalese traders generally set up their stalls, took out his 357 Magnum revolver and began to fire.

Revolver in hand, Casseri made his way back to his car. A news agent attempted to stop him but gave up when Casseri waved his gun at him. The gunman drove to kill again. This time at San Lorenzo Market. Casseri drove into the City centre and left his car in San Lorenzo underground car park. He then set off to hunt Senegalese again.

He located his first victim on one side of the old market square, which is lined with bars and restaurants. Casseri left him lying on the ground with four bullet wounds. After a brief pause to reload, the killer homed in on his second victim on the side of the square opposite the large covered market hall, near the corner of one of the lanes leading to Santa Maria Novella station. After that, Casseri went back to his car. Meanwhile, police and Carabinieri Officers had rushed to the area on foot, in cars, on motorbikes and even in helicopter. As they were organizing the evacuation of the zone, officers noticed Casseri in his car in the underground car park. One officer reacted with two shots at the car, striking the bodywork on the side opposite Casseri, who was in the passenger seat. Casseri then aimed his gun at his throat and pulled the trigger. The 357 Magnum bullet passed through his head and there was nothing more anyone could do.

The Victims the racist killer left were two dead Senegalese. Sambo Modou, 40 years old, and Diop Mor 54 years old were murdered by Gianluca Casseri in Piazza Dalmazia with a Smith and Wessen 357 Magnum revolver. Sambo Modou lived in Via Puccini in Sesto Fiorentino and Diop Mor lived in Via Primo Settembre. **"MAY THEIR GENTLE SOULS REST IN PERFECT PEACE WITH GOD ALMIGHTY IN JESUS NAME-AMEN"**.

THE WOUNDED - The other Senegalese shot in Piazza Dalmazzia is Moutapha Dieng, 34, who was admitted to Carregi hospital. Others seriously wounded were Sougou Mor, 32 years and Mbenghe Cheike, 42 years. In his attempts to defend himself, Mor, put up his arms to fend off the four 357Magnum bullets that were fired from close range. He stopped three, which broke his bones and the fourth struck him in the chest. Mor suffered multiple fractures and a chest injury.

Protesters after the shooting in France

Sougou Mor was taken first to the hospital at Santa Maria Nuova and then to Carreggi, where Doctors considered a chest operation during the night. However Moustapha

Dieng, the seriously wounded survivor of the first attack, could be left paralysed. Health care workers said that Dieng was hit by two bullets. One shot only grazed him but the other through his chest from a top-down angle, damaging two vertebrae.

AFRICANS MARCH - Many Africans who make living selling souvenirs (gifts) to tourists marched from Piazza Dalmazia and wound their way through the center of Florence. When the demonstrators were told that the murderer had shot himself, they demanded to see the body as proof. Some marchers knocked over Mopeds, road signs and waste bins near Santa Novella station.

When you are looking for housing and accommodation and you are an African, it poses a herculean task. They prefer a white skinned man in their neighbourhood. Black Africans live in poverty twice the rate among white people. Despite improving academic performance and qualification, they still face prejudice in job interviews and are paid lower wages than their white counterparts.

The most difficult, dangerous and dirty (DDD) jobs are done by the Africans. Occupational promotion is slow and some-times non existent for them. Wages and salaries paid to Africans do not commensurate with the jobs they do.

For 250 years Africans were kidnapped and taken for slavery. The family of Stephen Lawrence were descendants of ex-slaves from the continent of Africa. They incidentally landed in the Caribbean. Neville Lawrence 69, and Mrs Moreen Lawrence moved to Britain from Jamaica in the early 1960 and married in 1972. Two years later Stephen was born. On the 22nd of April 1993 Stephen was stabbed to death in an unprovocked attack at a bus stop on Well hall road in Eltham, South East London.

He was waiting at the bus-stop with his friend Duwayne Brooks to catch the bus going to his house in Woolwich when a gang of up to six white racist youths attacked him. One of the attackers shouted **"WHAT, WHAT NIGGER"**! and they all gave a chase. The gang surrounded Stephen, delivered two fatal knife blows and then fled. Stephen staggered to his feet and started to run. Stephen made it for about 20 metres along Well hall road before he Collapsed. Within 48 hours, numerous people had identified members of the Accourt gang as being responsible. Stephen was born on the 13th of September, 1974 and was murdered on the 22nd of April, 1993. **"MAY HIS SOUL REST IN PEACE IN JESUS NAME - AMEN."**

On Tuesday the 3rd of January 2012, Mr Justice Treacy convicted the duo of Gary Dobson and David Norris for the murder of Stephen Lawrence at Old Bailey. Mrs Moreen Lawrence received the conviction with mixed feelings. "How can I celebrate when my son lies buried? When I cannot see him or speak to him? When will I see him grow up and go to University or get married or have children? This verdict will not bring my son back", She sobbed. The mother of Stephen Lawrence has accused the Police of putting her through 18 years of grief and uncertainty.

Stephen was blessed with maturity and humuor. A decent and harmless black student who dreamed of being an Architect. He was a talented athlete who was an active member of Cambridge Harriers running Club. He was buried in Jamaica, the country his parents left in 1960's in search of a better life.

However, UK Daily Mail of 16th of March, 2013 has published the admission story by Doreen. For 20 years Dobson denied any part in the racist killing of Stephen Lawrence. But finally after a private prosecution, landmark inquiry, years of police investigations, and a murder conviction, Gary Dobson admitted his guilt. On the 15th of March, 2013 Gary Dobson abandoned his appeal and admitted his guilt. Dobson's decision was welcomed by Stephen's mother - Doreen. In a moving statement, she spoke of the pain and heart break of the years she has spent waiting for his confession.

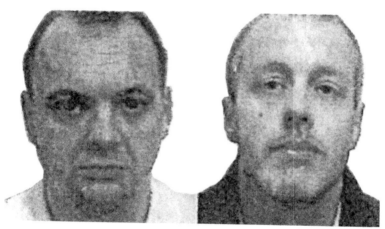

Gary Dobson   David Norris

If Stephen had been carrying Marijuana that night it is a fair bet that the whole case would have drifted into obscurity as "drug related". But he wasn't. So the killing ended Britain's denial about racism. Racism is exhibited in all ramifications of life against black Africans especially in sports, modeling, in the school system, against the growth of churches, in the media, in politics, etc.

RACISM IN SPORTS

Although it has received plenty of attention for many years, racism still plagues certain sports. No sport is immune, but some appear to attract racist and xenophobic behaviour more than others. Football is the sport with most obvious difficulties. The English and German football leagues administration have been trying to stamp out racist slurs and monkey chants but ugly incidents continue to happen. In 2007, the English Football Association announced that it would investigate allegations of racist abuse by Newcastle United fans against the Middlesborough striker, Mido. He is currently retired from professional football and is coaching Zamalek of Egypt.

Samuel Eto'o

Samuel Eto'o who is currently in chelsea Football club of England had the same problem while in Barcelona. In Barcelona football club, he had a running battle with racist fans chanting and hurling racist abuse at him. Due to ongoing racism from Laliga crowds when he was playing for Barcelona football club, Eto'o stopped bringing family members to matches. Eto'o complained that racism has affected him personally and he suggested that players, leaders and the media have to join forces so that no one feels looked down upon on account of race. Eto'o along with former teammates Thierry Henry and Universitatea Craiova defender, Marco Zoro have several times reacted by being outspoking in protest and threatened to leave the pitch.

Peter Osaze Odemwingie is currently in Stoke city of England. While in West Bromwich Albion, Osaze and his country Nigeria had problems when he was leaving Locomotive Moscow football club. While he was with Locomotiv Moscow he did a lot for them. With immence power and pace, he was the driving force of the attack and one of their most important players.

Osaze Odemwingie

Shortly after signing for West Brom in the United Kingdom, Locomotive fans were celebrating the sale of Odemwingie through the use of racist banners targeted at the player. One banner included the image of a BANANA and read- "

THANKS WEST BROM". Though his mother is Russian, the racist fans did not consider Osaze ethnically Russian. The racist fans forgot that our brother is not a slave player. He has every right to leave and play for any football club anywhere in the world.

Football Against Racism in Europe (FARE) says that the willingness of a governing body to get involved in addressing the problem is crucial. Many football associations are reluctant to sign up to FARE campaigns against racism. Politicians should be on board to draft legislation and form education policies.

Congolese footballer, Zola Matumona dropped his complaint of racism against FC Brussel's boss Johann Vermeersch, and the two called a press conference to announce their reconciliation. Vermeersch was said to have taunted Matumona, telling him to climb a tree to eat a bunch of bananas.

In England, Paul Ince at MK Dons and Keith Alexander at Macclesfield are the first and only black managers of the 92 premier and football league clubs according to Daily Telegraph UK of March 12, 2008. Ryan Giggs can still recall when bananas were thrown at John Barnes while playing for Liverpool in a match against Everton.

Mario Balotelli is now with Ac milan of italy. While he was Manchester city talisman, he is seen here protesting racist chanting against him as he raised his jersey to reveal the words- " WHY IS IT ALWAYS ME?" He revealed this words inscribed in his inner shirts during the Barclays League football match played on Sunday the 23rd of October, 2011 at the Manchester City stadium. Manchester City aka- "the citizens"- engaged their city rival Manchester United Football club in which Mario Balotelli scored two goals of the 6-1 bashing of Manchester United.

Striker Mario Balotelli, was abused during an international friendly. Balotelli, the first black player to be picked for Italy was booed by his own team's supporters during a clash against Romanian. During the game, a banner was held up saying-'**NO TO A MULTI-RACIAL ITALIAN TEAM**. Palermo born Balloteli has Ghanaian heritage and made a high pro-file £24 million move from Inter Milan to Manchester City in August, 2010.In October, 2011 during a football match Lius Suarez a Liverpool Striker clashed and racially abused Patrice Evra, a Manchester United defender. According to Nigerian Flagship Newspaper, *THE GUARDIAN* of Monday 16th of January, 2012 Evra the Manchester United defender had reportedly asked the Uruguayan Luis Suarez why he was taking delight in constantly kicking him whenever the two contested for the ball. **"BECAUSE YOU ARE BLACK"** was the reported reply from the Uruguayan. When Evra threatened to respond in kind if the kicking continued, Suarez replied, **"I DO NOT TALK TO BLACK AFRICANS"**, in a deplorable reference to Evra's skin colour.

Mario Baloteli

The Uruguayan also mockingly and derogatorily used Spanish to call Evra- 'NEGRO'. Lius Suarez speaks Spanish and NEGRO in Spanish Means- 'BLACK'. Any insultive reference to the colour of any person must not only be condemned but also be punished. Suarez was charged for racism. The Football Association (FA) investigative body went to work, and the result was a startling 115 page document which exposed the whole truth, as Suarez was indicted for racially abusing Evra as many as seven times within two minutes during the match. On the strength of the overwhelming evidence against the Uruguayan, the England FA confirmed the eight game ban and a £40,000 fine imposed on Luis Suarez.

There was a flashpoint incident in the 85th minute of Queens Park Rangers (QPR) surprise 1-0 win over Chelsea in a match that was played on October 23rd at Loftus road QPR stadium. John Terry who doubles as the Chelsea and England football Captain had cast a racial Slur. He racially abused Anton Ferdinand a black of African descent who plays for QPR. John Terry mouthed the words - "YOU FUCKING BLACK" which irritated Anton Ferdinand. Anton met Queens Park Rangers Manager Neil Warnock and complained bitterly. Anton is the brother of England football vice captain Rio Ferdinand.

Monday November 7th, 2011, English newspaper, The Sun carried the headline "Death Threat to Race Row Ace". The follow up story was a report from the police investigating a terrifying death threat against race row soccer star Anton Ferdinand. Anton was told by the police to fit a panic alarm at his home.

Worried Police Officers told Anton Ferdinand to fix alarm which connects to the Police if he is facing imminent attack from racist fans. Worried Officers acted after reading a letter sent to

Queens Park Rangers club on the 4th of November, 2011. The details in the threat note were so frightening and graphic that cops told Anton and other close relatives they must take immediate precautionary measures. Some family members have already taken the advice and installed the alarms. They are a direct connection to a nearby station and mean police car can arrive in minutes. The letter threatening Anton was delivered to QPR's ground by hand on Friday the 4th of November, 2011. Because of the detail, club Bosses decided Anton Ferdinand should not see it. A police spokesman said "we confirm we are investigating an Allegation of malicious communication".

Anton Ferdinand and
John Terry: Confrontation

Anton continued to wear anti- racism T-shirt after the incident. Rio who was 32 years old and the elder brother of Anton also wore a **"UNITED AGAINST RACISM"** arm band during his team's 2-0 champions league win over Otelul Galati of Turkey. This did not stop supporters of John Terry who were clearly and repeatedly heard chanting **"ANTON FERDINAND-YOU KNOW WHAT YOU ARE"** in their 1-1 group E draw at the Cristal Arena in a match played at stadion plein 4, 3600 in Genk, Belgium.

Again football's racism row took a sinister new twist on Friday January 27, 2012 when a maniac posted a shotgun cartridge to Anton Ferdinand. The QPR defender opened the hate-filled package at the club's training ground at Harrington, West London. It was also said to contain a threatening letter addressed to the star.

John Terry

John Terry, a leader of his football club (Chelsea) and country, was five months away from captaining England in the European championship finals when the telephone rang at 10 am Friday the 3rd of February, 2012. The £170,000 a week Chelsea defender was informed of his sack by David Bernstein the chairman of the Football Association. The FA had come under mounting pressure from footballers, including Jason Roberts and Piara Power, the head of "Football Against Racism In Europe (FARE)". Apart from the pressure mounted by footballers and ex-footballers, the FA felt that captain Terry standing among certain black team- mates has been diminished by allegation that he racially abused Anton Ferdinand and decided to stripe him of the armband before his trial in July, 2012 on racially aggravated public order offence. The FA Board voted against him. The England captaincy was incredibly important to him, in many ways a validation of his career and commitment.

With John Terry's trial, football and race were in the dock. Five days ordeal at Westminister magistrates court ended shortly after 2pm on Friday the 13th of July, 2012. They are not guilty verdict in the trial of John Terry was greeted with anger and bemusement by the black African community in Britain. The decision could deter players who have been racially abused from coming forward in the future.

The judge, Mr Riddle exhaustive judgement declared "weighing all the evidence together.... I accept it is possible that Mr Terry believed at the time and now that accusation of racism was made". He said TV footage did not show the complete exchange of words. Meaning it was impossible to be sure exactly what was said. No doubt John Terry uttered the words f****** black c**** at Anton Ferdinand. Mr Riddles comments appear to make Terry liable to an FA charge that saw Liverpool Luis Suarez fined £40,000 and banned for eight games.

You can see from the above story that Britain is fairly a good country to be in as a black African when compared to some European countries. However, national connivance and denial had continously obscured the reality of British racism.

Police on Thursday the 2nd of February, 2012 probed a race hate campaign against Newcastle United striker Shola Ameobi after "sickening" messages targeted at him were posted on Facebook. Officers reported the matter and detectives tried to find the culprit. A Newcastle spokesman said- "we have a zero tolerance approach to racism and will always seek to take the strongest possible action". In November, 2011 Ameobi younger brother Sammy, 19 who also plays for Newcastle, was sent vile abuse on Twitter.

Black football stars like Jason Roberts, Stan Collymore, Rio Ferdinand and Darren Byfield were at one time or the other deluged with vile racist abuse. According to the London newspaper- The TIMES of Wednesday 28, 2012, a student named Liam Stacey was jailed for 56 days for tweeting racist comments about Fabrice Muamba after the footballer collapsed from a heart attack.

Fabrice Muamba

He tweeted the racist comments as the Bolton Wanderers midfielder Lay on the pitch during an FA cup tie against Tottenham Hotspur on March 17, 2012 as millions watched his fight for life. Instead of showing concern Stacey took to Twitter to mock the African player. Stacey tweets reads: LOL (LAUGH OUT LOUD) F*** Muamba. He's dead!!!. He then posted a series of racist comments. The offence is clearly racially aggravated. There was sustained and gratuitous racism. Stacey, from Pontypridd, south Wales, addmitted inciting racial hatred in a brief appearance at Swansea Magistrates Court.

CHRISTOPHER SAMBA the ex- Blackburn Rovers player and Congolese defender spoke out after a banana was thrown at him during Anzhi Makhachkala's 1-0 defeat to Locomotive Moscow on Sunday afternoon the 25th of March, 2012. A banana came down at Samba from the VIP section as the team was leaving the field. Samba picked the banana and threw it back to the VIP section. Despite Samba speaking out on the incident, Locomotive president, Olga Smorodskaya issued a denial to the Russian media after the match. "This did not happen, and could not have happened", she said.

There is no hiding place for Christopher Samba when it comes to racial attack. On his return from Russia to play again in the English premiership, he signed for Queens' Park Rangers. When his club was hosted in a match by Fulham FC, a racist twitter called him "NEGRO".

Christopher Samba

England hero Sol Campbell told of his battle with football racists as he met the parents of murdered black US teen, Trayvon Martin on Thursday the 10th of May, 2012. The Ex-Spurs and Arsenal defender said he was taunted with monkey chants on the pitch throughout his glittering career.

Sol spoke out as he met Tracey Martin, 45 and 46 year old Sybrina Fulton whose unarmed son Trayvon, 17, was shot by neighbourhood watch Chief, George Zimmerman at a gated community near Orlando, Florida in February, 2012. Speaking of his own Experiences of racism, he said: "If he was a white footballer he would have been treated differently". He said one of the worst times was at Sunderland. Every time he touched the ball he had heard monkey chants. He could not believe it. He was just 19 or 20 years old player and it was a big shock. Those stories keep coming up. The ugly head keeps rising.

Even the popular football player Didier Drogba is not spared racism attack. The London Metro newspaper of Thursday 3rd of May, 2012 on page 5 carried a report of racial abuse perpetrated against Didier Drogba. The racist Chelsea fan was banned from football matches for three years after he racially abused his team striker Didier Drogba. Stephen Fitzwater was watching in the stadium the FA cup semi-final match played on Sunday the 15th of April, 2012 when he was heard aiming a racist slur at the Player. The 55 year old from Isleworth, west London, admitted racially aggravated abuse at Hendon Magistrates' Court. He was also banned for life by Chelsea.

In the summer of 2012, European football championship was co-hosted by Poland and Ukraine. Fear of racism affected the game. Black England players such as Arsenal's Alex Oxlade Chamberlain and Theo Walcott had said their families will not travel to watch the matches to avoid racist attack. Also racism in Poland and Ukraine gave Italian international player Balotelli much worry. Balotelli has vowed to kill any racist hooligan that dare throw banana at him during the competition.

Didier Drogba

Despite the warning threat to kill any racist who dare throw banana at him prior to the competition, Balotelli was the target of monkey chants and had a banana thrown at him during his side's 1-1 draw with the Croatia in Poznan on Thursday the 14th of June, 2012. According to The Evening Standard of Tuesday 19th June, 2012 a steward picked up a banana which was allegedly thrown at Balotelli by Croatia supporters when he was substituted. Croatia coach said "I do not like these kind of supporters. This is a big problem around the world. I am really disappointed with this as a parent, and as a sportsman. Balotelli was also racially abused by Spain fans during their 1-1 draw in Gdansk on Sunday the 10th of June, 2012.

Dutch black players also complained of racist chanting aimed at them during a training session in Krakow. Russian fans allegedly abused the Czech republic's Theodor Gebre Selassie who is of Ethiopian origin. Friday the 21st of September, 2012 Roberto Di Matteo criticised twitter users who sent racist messages to John Mikel Obi following his mistake in the 2-2 draw with Juventus on Wednesday the 19th of September, 2012.

Mikel who gave the ball away in the build-up to Juventus leveler, closed his twitter account apparently in response to the racist comments. The club reported two incidents of totally unacceptable, disgusting and abhorrent abuse to Police. It vowed to ban any fan that engaged in such behavior. Mikel Obi was racially abused by referee Mark Clattenburg when Chelsea football Club played Manchester United in the Capital One Cup. Two Chelsea stars are believed to have told team mates they heard referee Clattenburg tell Mikel- **"SHUT UP, YOU MONKEY"**.

'MONKEY'

What ref is alleged to have called black Chelsea star Mikel

Senegalese Winger El Hadji Diouf when he was at leeds united was racially abused by Millwall Football club fans in November, 2012. He was racially abused about 56 times during the match between Leeds United and Millwall football club at the New Den. Under cover report has found El

Hadji Diouf was called "Slave" and "Nigger" by five white supporters of Millwall football club. The match played on the 18th of November, 2012 was won by Millwall yet EL-Hadji Diouf was targeted for racial taunting.

EL-Hadji Diouf

Yaya Toure the Ivory Coast midfielder was racially abused by opposition fans on Wednesday October 23, 2013 during Manchester City 2-1 win against CSKA Moscow in Russia. Monkey chants were directed towards Toure during the game. Toure, Manchester City's Captain in the absence of Vincent Kompany and a fluent Russian speaker reported the incident to Ovidiu Hategan,the referee

Yaya Toure

from Romania.Toure said it is unbelievable and very sad on his part.

"As an African player it is always sad when you hear some-thing like that". he said Toure went as far as urging UEFA to consider closing the Khimki Arena, CSKA's home ground, for up to a couple of years until the problem is eradicated. The 30 year old post-match comments went into greater detail, revealing his hurt at being targeted because he is African. Toure turned to Twitter, stating Yaya Toure says no to racism.

In some football (soccer) matches I have watched, white footballers while in possession of the ball in the vital area (goal area) often hesitate to pass to black players that are freer and better positioned to score the goals. While giving a radio interview Wigan Athletic Chairman, Dave Whelan suggested that black African players should just continue playing and not complain if they are subjected to racial abuse. Unfortunately, I find Whelan's comments too appalling,degrading, preposterious, impudent and callous to hear. Black African sportsmen and women plying their trade in the diaspora must continue to voice their anger against racism in all its ramifications.

But football is not the only sport to have suffered such incidents. During the American Vietnam war, Muhammad Ali, formally known as Casius Clay, ex- world heavy weight boxing champion refused conscription into the U.S. army. Muhammad Ali a native of Louisville, Kentucky was targeted for conscription more because he was a rising black star than on his religious beliefs. In 1967, Muhammad Ali's boxing license was seized. He was banned from participating in the heavy weight championship for refusing to fight in the Vietnam war. He fought tooth and nail before he could regain his boxing license. After regaining his license, he concentrated on his boxing career which eventually flourished.

Racism in rugby has also been creeping into Europe, Asia and America. Sports with big appeal such as basketball have had similar problems. In the U.S., black sports men and women are often caught in a dilemma when teams lose, they are unfairly blamed for being responsible, if they win, they hardly get any praise.

RACISM IN MODELLING

There is a racist culture in modeling agencies. The fashion world has sidelined black African beauties. There is a dearth of black African models on the front of glossy magazines since supermodel Naomi Campbell appeared on the front of British Vogue in August, 2002. But since then no African model has been similarly promoted. It is a pity that publishers of these magazines and modelling agencies do not appreciate black beauty even Naomi has said that she gets a raw deal from her own country, England. She hardly gets on the front pages of London magazines. Only white models, some of whom are not as prominent as she are put on splash pages. Black models do not get equal prominence and recognition by the world media. Models with light skin are more likely to advance with their careers.

Supermodel Naomi Campbell attacked the fashion world for failing to employ more black models. While receiving a special Recognition award at the recent British Fashion Awards ceremony, campbell said: "We are aware that we need to introduce more women of colour". Supermodel Naomi Campbell told a British News station that she believes fashion designers are snubbing black models. She said the act of not choosing models of colour is racist.

Naomi Campbell

Naomi Campbell stated that she called Victoria Beckham in person at the height of the row over race discrimination in the fashion world. Campbell launched a high profile campaign to expose discrimination on the catwalk and identified Victoria Beckham's company as being on the "accused guilty list". Victoria was being criticized for using

Victoria Beckham

only one non- white model in her 30 strong London Fashion Week show. Campbell, who is spearheading the anti-racism Diversity Coalition with David Bowie's model wife, Iman, wrote an open letter to fashion bosses in London, New York, Paris and Milan.

The letter pointed out that at New York Fashion Week only 6 per cent of models were Black and that fewer black models are used now than in the Seventies. It went on to list fashion houses guilty of this racist act including Victoria Beckham, Calvin Klein, Donna Karan, Roberto Cavalli, Chanel, Armani, Gucci, Saint Laurent, and Marc Jacobs. Campbell has defended her actions, saying "there is no way to candy coat this sort of Thing. You have to be straight. We had the percentages and we were armed with the facts. I have spoken the truth, people might not like it", she said.

Sola Oyebade, owner of Europe's largest modeling agency believes that the paucity in the use of black models is down to companies believing black African models cannot sell as well as their white counterparts. "They don't really want to use black models anyway because they say 'black does not sell'. Discrimination is commonplace in the modeling industry, as more than a third of fashion weeks in London, Paris, Milan and New York did not feature any black models. African models should know the fact that the fashion industry does not have a fair cultural representation on the catwalk, magazines and on billboards.

Beyonce

In 2005, singer Beyonce Knowles was caught up in a controversy after appearing on the front cover of Vanity Fair, when the magazine was accused of air brushing her image to make her skin appear lighter. You do not really see black models on the front covers of mainstream magazines. The black models you do see tend to have features that are less ethical and more Europeanised. You hardly ever see a black model in the public eye. According to UK Independent newspaper of Monday December 17, 2007, "There is a lack of black faces on the catwalk".

INSTITUTIONAL RACISM IN THE SCHOOL SYSTEM

In Europe, Asia and America, there exists institutional racism in schools. African boys were three times more likely to be permanently excluded from schools than white youngsters. African boys and white boys might have committed the same offence, but the African is always indicted for punishment. There is rarely social cohesion. In Britain, schools wriggle to get out of taking in poor kids from Africa. They narrow their catchment areas and set up bogus tests of academic skills. A lot of the African kids fail these deliberately bogus tests and are pushed out of the white schools. This means these kids pile up in the worst schools where they become unteachable. According to the BBC television report monitored in May, 2012 the reporter Susanna Reid reported that 80,000 incidents of racist abuse were recorded in the past four years in English Schools. African teachers and teaching assistants are often bullied, spat on, jeered at, mocked and hekled by white students. They create very unconducive atmosphere to frustrate teaching. Teaching assistants of African origin are subjected to horrific abuse by white students. Most of them often suffered physical attack.

In October, 2011, I was assigned to invigilate Mathematics examination at Rokeby (Boys) school on Barking Road, Newham in London. During the examination, a white student rudely and loudly asked me what grade I made in my Ordinary Level GCSE Mathematics. What a disparaging and insultive question! I was dumfounded and embarrassed. Though I made A in my GCSE Mathematics, it would have been stupid of me to tell the student my grade.

RACISM AGAINST BLACK CHURCHES
Across Europe and America, black Africans' majority churches face a new wave of racism from town halls that are rejecting bids to build new premises. Expanding congregations have made many churches victims of their own success as they outgrow rented schools, cinema houses and community halls. Some have ended up homeless.

Many churches that have raised funds to build new places of worship were failing to get planning permission from their local town halls. They stereotype black churches.The stereotype is- "black people always coming together and praising the Lord with noisy choirs". They protest that the noise they generate from the churches destabilizes their immediate communities. No native European or American considers the fact that black people put a lot back into their communities. Councils tend to be white and middle class and so the black majority churches have no representation sitting on their local government councils to raise their problems for discussion and solution. No wonder this is seen as a race issue.

Bishop Nicholson says his Croydon based church in London is battling to stay in its place of worship, despite occupying the building for more than five years. Kingsway International Christian Centre (KICC), the biggest black church in Europe was also denied planning permission in February, 2008. KICC had agreed to move from its previous premises because it was within the 2012 Olympic site.

The church submitted a planning application to Havering Council and the London Thames Gateway Development Corporation (LTGDC) in association with the London Development Agency for a new church, but they were refused. Pastor Dipo Oluyomi, chief executive of KICC, said the Havering site remained the only viable option for meeting their unique needs. "This is a perfect illustration of authorities prejudice against black African Christianity. If KICC was an entertainment complex, you can be sure they would have been treated more sympathetically especially if its management were white".

RACISM IN THE MEDIA

In the western media both print and electronic, the visual images of Africa are potent-tattered clothing, starving babies and children, machetes, guns, rape and famine. They do not mention that Africa is still the place where multinationals like Shell, Chevron, etc. derive their coal, oil, gas, uranium, gold, diamonds, copper and other strategic minerals.

The western media serves as the propaganda arm of their governments. It is rare to find balance in the media. Since I have been living in Europe for over twenty years, I can count how many times I have watched a Western Television report about my home country Nigeria, if they report anything, they report about slums but my country is definitely more than that. Its not just slums ! Why can't they show the positive side as well? They portray Africans as objects of ridicule. For us living abroad, we are confronted daily by the endemic western media stereotyping of Africans which has reinforced and crystallised an image of a people so pervasive and profound,with intractable problems.

During the 2012 US presidential campaign, majority of western media overtly or covertly ganged up against the re-election of President Hussein Barack Obama. Africans in general and Africans in the Diaspora in particular will see no respite from the negative stereotypical reports by the western media unless Africans develop their own media houses (print and electronics) to counter western media ugly reports of Africa and Africans in the Diaspora.

Africa media houses will certainly project to the world good images of Africa and Africans in the Diaspora. The creation of African media houses across Asia, Australasia, Europe and the Americas is a welcome development. Here in the UK, there exist a plethora of radio stations that cater to the wish of African ethnic nationalities. The establishment of Television stations like BEN Television, Vox Africa, OHTV, etc. is highly applauded. There also exist ethnic nationality Newspapers like the TRIUMPH, the monthly NIGERIAN WATCH, SOUTH AFRICA, UGANDA and KENYA Newspapers here in the UK.

RACISM IN POLITICS
Britain's top black weekly newspaper, THE VOICE, carried a report written by Dapo Oyebanji on its 14-20 June, 2012 edition. It reported that Diane Abbot, UK Member of Parliament (MP) representing Hackney North and Stoke Newington was in the 1980's constantly asked "how could a black woman represent white people?" When she ran many black people were doubtful. They simply could not imagine a black person as a United Kingdom Member of Parliament.

When Martin Luther King gave his "dream speech" in 1963, he proclaimed his desire to see an America which would hold "self-evident", that all men are created equal. The historic August 28 **"I HAVE A DREAM SPEECH"** at the March on Washington was delivered at the world war memorial Chicago Soldier field. He lambasted the racist establishment, declaring that nobody should judge a man by the colour of his skin but rather by the quality of his character.

Unfortunately, having an African- American president in the person of Barack Obama does not mean all people believe that to be possible. To fend off racial prejudice during his campaign 2008 he harped on the slogan "Yes We Can" by extension he means, "Black Man Can ". The American establishment feels that a black man can not be entirely trusted with a very high position of responsibility. For fear of rejection and castigation, Obama coined the parlance to assuage the prejudice prevailing in the land.

In 1995, when it seemed Colin Powell might run for president, Powell explained his appeal to white voters thus: "I speak reasonably well like a white person, and visually I aint that black". Even President Obama owed his success in part to "light skinned "appearance and the fact that he spoke with no Negro accent. That Obama possessed these qualities were not even enough, he still had to fight tooth and nail against racial hatred towards him and his race, the African race.

THE OATH TAKING SAGA

The inauguration of Barack Obama as the 44th President of the USA, which took place on Tuesday January 20, 2009 was unprecedented in the annals of American history. It was an epoch making event because Obama broke the record as the first ever black man to be elected and sworn in as the first black president of America. Chief Justice John Roberts administered the oath of office of the President of the United States to Obama. His wife, Michelle held the Bible used by Abraham Lincoln at his 1861 inauguration, as Obama placed his hand on the bible to recite the presidential oath.

During the swearing in ceremony, Obama did not recite and Roberts, as the administering official, did not execute the 35 word oath of office exactly as prescribed by the United States Constitution. The first mistake occurred during the first part of the oath when without waiting for Roberts to finish the first phrase, Obama began reciting the oath.

After the correct recitation of the first phase, Roberts recited incorrectly the next part of the oath by saying "that I will faithfully execute the office of president to the United States faithfully", rather than, "that I will faithfully execute the office of President of the United States". Obama knew that Roberts had made a mistake and he paused but this is no mistake but a deliberate action. It would have been an open question whether Obama is the president until he takes the proper oath.

White House counsel had to pressure Chief Justice Roberts to retake the oath. Can you imagine that a second oath ceremony took place on that evening of January 21, 2009 in the Map Room of the White House before a small audience of presidential aides, reporters and a White House photographer. The presidential oath had to be retaken over concerns about the legality of the oath as it was administered on inauguration day. Why was the oath so shabbily administered in the first place? The answer is obvious in that it is when unconventionality clashes with conventionality. It is unconventional and unthinkable that a black man is sworn in as the president.

Did you know that no bible was present during the retaking of the oath at the inauguration, which aroused some criticisms. Washington political hawks find it difficult to come to terms with the fact that a black man was sworn in as president of the greatest nation on earth.

Action needed

Diane Abbott

Barack Obama taking oath as president of the United State of America

The election of the first black president of the United States raised expectations and uncertainties about how America would perhaps for the first time in a while, begin to wrestle with the question of race. Would Obama's presidency lead to unprecedented enlightenment, respect and candour around the topic of race? Would it provoke a backlash and release an uglier more shameful conversation generally held in private? Would it fulfill the hopes and dreams of the civil rights movements? Would it lead to a rush by white Americans to acquire more black friends?

Since the inauguration of President Obama, American attitudes toward race and the conversation around the topic have remained obstinately the same. By some accounts the situation may even be worse.

The Washington Post of 18th January, 2010 reported on a poll it conducted with ABC News which concluded that soaring expectations about the effect of the first black president of the USA race relations have collided with a more mundane reality. According to the poll, the percentage of Americans who think Obama's presidency will improve race relations has dropped from 58% just before his inauguration to 41% one year later. People now realize that the election of Obama has not resolved 400 years of history. Obama poll victory was a huge redemptive moment for African-Americans. But the problem of inequality still persists. Optimism among blacks has decreased since his election from 50% to 20%.

Despite often channeling the words of Martin Luther King Junior during his speeches, President Obama is still limited by his ethnic origin. Obama won due to a confluence of factors: opposition to the Iraq war; a disciplined campaign that took advantage of a pre-existing movement for change; the personality ambition; intellectual and communications skills to ride that wave; and an incumbent party that had been in the White House for eight long years and which had unleashed a politician of mass destruction especially as regard his violation of Kyoto protocol on climate change – BUSH.

Early on in Obama's candidacy, there were stated resistance to him from the black community. Established civil rights leaders ignored or minimised him. Black radio hosts challenged his racial bonafides. Black people did not take Obama seriously, but when he won in Iowa, the racial discourse that set in shortly after that victory, set the stage for what we would see in his presidency.

Since that victory, people of colour, especially blacks, have had to constantly fight to be seen as legitimate members of US communities. They now strive to legitimise their existence in the USA. Despite incredible sacrifice and tangible measures of patriotism (e.g. military enlistment), Black Americans are always under threat of being cast as outsiders.

Ten official inaugural balls (dance party) followed his historic inauguration. During the inauguration, the celebration headlines screamed- "Obama overcomes", "Obama makes history", "Obama shatters racial barriers", "A new dawn", "The first black man president", "An African-American president" and other similarly epic phrases .

We had done "it", although it was never fully articulated just what "it" was. For a few months, the Republican opposition was silent, but now they have driven up irrational opposition to many of the president's initiatives. Right wing talk show hosts are now lambasting Obama from every corner. They claim that Obama was elected by mostly black racists and white guilty people.

They claim that Obama's entire economic program is reparations and that he is a Marxist who wants to take almost everything from the super rich white class to fund the health care of the lazy black people.

President Barack Obama and first lady Michelle
at the inaugural parade in 2009

Large crowds at the inauguration of Barack Obama as President of USA

President Barack Obama and his wife at the inauguration venue

Spectators watch on large screen

Crowd of people as Barack Obama takes the oath as the 44 president of the United States of America

President Barack Obama and wife at the Inaugural Ball in Washington, DC.

First dance as President

President Barack .H.Obama greets guest after swearing
in as a 44th president of the United States of America

They also say that President Obama has exposed himself as a man who, over and over again, has deep seated hatred for white people, or the white culture. He is giving too much hard working white peoples' money to lazy people of colour mainly people of African descent.

Hence the Massachusetts election shocker. The republicans rallied round and voted overwhelmingly for Scot Brown, who defeated the democratic candidate Martha Coakley, the candidate from the traditional democratic stronghold where the Kennedys held sway. Because of the defeat of Coakley, it is possible that the great hope of extending medical coverage to tens of millions of uninsured black Americans may have died with President Obama's election.

As the 41st republican in the 100 member chamber, Mr Brown promises to use his vote to deprive and frustrate the democrats of the filibuster supermajority vote they had been depending on. In Washington DC, as in Massachusetts, the democrats were slow to see the possibility of this remarkable reversal. Now because of this negative political scenario, there is political dangers to his presidency.

President Obama knows that because of racism and the fact that the white people dominate the population of America, his re-election will be very difficult. So he made a face saving statement saying that he would rather be a really good one term president than a mediocre two term one, he told ABC's World News anchor, Diane Sawyer, in an exclusive interview on Monday 25th January, 2010. Fortunately, President Hussein Barrack Obama has been voted again to govern United States of America for another four years. The re-election has gone a long way to re-affirm the Parlance - "YES WE CAN".

CHAPTER SEVEN

Future Aspiration of Africans Living Abroad

In the short term, new African migrants to Europe, America and Asia are likely to enter a world of detention camps surrounded by barbed wire while the authorities deliberate over their future. Some are deported although removing them to their home countries can be difficult if they arrive without documents. Some on Spanish or Italian islands will be transferred to the mainland where they will hope to be released by authorities powerless to deport them or detain them for long.

The likelihood is that they will join the vast army of illegal workers fuelling their nations of residence economy but barred from using its services. There is a big question mark hanging over the heads of these army of African immigrants. And that is, if the future is sure and bright for African immigrants living in foreign countries.

When an African sets his or her foot on European or American or Asian soil, he or she looses a lot of his or her rights and privileges. He or she could be classified as second class citizen, the underdog, the underprivileged, the dregs of society, etc. Often, there is one rule for the natives and another for the migrants especially African migrants, ranging from rules on housing, education, job opportunities, wages and salaries and economic well being, civil rights, justice systems, etc.

There is always a glass ceiling placed above the heads of every African migrant struggling to climb the social ladder. Which ever profession you find yourself in, you can hardly break through this hard glass ceiling. Most of the time your overall boss has to be an indigen of the host country - so no matter your intelligence, your energy, or your wittiness, you might not be judged by these attributes. And no matter the input and effort into your job, you can hardly be recommended to head any department you may find yourself in. The natives are groomed to be supervisors and administrators.

No matter your level of educational attainment, African migrants are pushed behind to do more laborious and menial jobs. They are the last to be hired and the first to be fired. Your ability to climb the social ladder is often constrained by a lot of encumbrances placed on you and on your ways. Laws are designed and often skewed to favour the indigenous people more than the 'unwanted' Africans.

Now, the European Commission is to take a stake in an EU wide quota for workers coming from countries that are sources of large numbers of illegal immigrants. They have unveiled plans to allow skilled workers to come to Europe for a limited period before returning to their home countries.

Bosses of companies and parastatals could face jail for hiring illegal workers. Employers who hire illegal African workers could face fines, exclusion from public funds and even jail, under plans which European commission unveiled on May 16th, 2006.

Illegal Africans are afraid to lodge complaints against employers and are often deported without their outstanding wages, taxes and social security contributions are paid out.

Criminal sanctions will apply to employers who repeatedly hire illegal workers.

Company outlets where offences take place can be closed down permanently or temporarily and employers excluded from any public money or from participating in public contracts for up to five years.

Employers will have to pay back any public money, aid or European Union subsides paid during the year prior to the discovery of the illegal employment. Employers will also have to pay for the costs of returning the illegal workers to their home countries. Tourism, public works and agriculture are the main areas where labour shortages would exist in the US and EU as the plan would see workers returning back to Africa when such seasonal work would finish.

For years, African immigrants have been the vegetable pickers, the street sweepers, the bus-boys, the ditch-diggers of the continents. They are the people straining to grab hold of the lowest rung of the economic ladder in the rich societies on earth. The money they send home is vital to the economies of their families, their villages and their countries.

CHAPTER EIGHT

The Yawning Social Gap Between African Migrants and Citizens of their Host Countries

There is a growing appetite to search for the best possible models of integration, citizenship and the balance of rights and responsibilities for the host nations and the Africans. Within the European Union for instance, co-operation on integration policies is essentially non-existent. Many European countries have failed to implement the race equality and employment directives that should be tackling discrimination mainly in the labour market on the grounds of race.

In the Church of St Boniface, less than two kilometres from the European parliament in Brussels, there are 130 asylum seekers taking sanctuary. I spoke with a Sudanese, who preferred to remain anonymous, who said they have no rights, no insurance, no identity and they have nothing to show for themselves. If they get caught by the police they get put back in closed centre for two months, all for nothing. You are not allowed to go out.

The problem is that they cannot go to any other country. They are stuck there. They cannot move - having been finger printed, they cannot leave Belgium. One Ibrahim, from Somalia, for instance, managed to get to the UK and was granted entry after undergoing an interview but he was later called in by the home office, arrested and sent back to Belgium following notification from the Belgium authorities. That is the lot of African immigrants everywhere - to be needed but not wanted.

Most undocumented African immigrants sleep rough - where drunk people would come up to them and harass them with racist comments. Most African refugees are condemned to destitution - they parade themselves as second class citizens.

African migrants are employed in appalling conditions and are paid below the national minimum wage. They live in squalor and wallow in abject poverty while their white counterparts swim in an ocean of opulence. The whites enjoy paid exotic holidays, good cars, fancy homes, etc. Children of African immigrants suffer from social exclusion. They take solace in dealing in cocaine, alcohol, sexual abuse, violent crime, etc.

Because of the vicious circle of poverty they are enmeshed in, they can ill afford to pay for new things. They are engulfed in second hand syndrome - they deal in overused clothes, cars, shoes, lorries, fridges, carpets, cutlery, handbags, traveling bags, jewellery, hoovers, mowers, washing machines, hairdryers, etc.

EDUCATIONAL RESTRICTION

In most parts of America and Europe, white parents remove their children from struggling schools which are often dominated by children from African backgrounds. Even if the schools are a stone throw from their houses, they remove the children to schools which are attended by majority of white children. The rejected schools groom average or mediocre children who often struggle to achieve barely 2 GCSE papers at credit levels.This tells on their admission prospects into tertiary institutions.

As a result of poor grade achievement, children of African parents carry an air of inferiority complex. As a consequence, they suffer from low self esteem and they lack self confidence. They are pigeon holed and bandied around negative stereotypes. There is also inequality among teaching staff. In the UK for example, black teachers, though as qualified as the natives, constitute 7.4% teaching staff, 4.9% managerial staff and 1% principals - according to The Voice, August 2007.

LIBERTY RESTRAINED
Often times Africans are arrested, prosecuted, abandoned or imprisoned. The prisons across Europe and America are mainly populated by children and adults of African origin. This ugly situation can only be rectified through a total overhaul of the justice system. Unless there is a turn around of the law in favour of Africans, the yawning social gap can never close.

THE RACIST ROLE OF THE WESTERN MEDIA
The western media portray Africans in a bad light. They ignore the good aspects of our national development and continental progress. Since I have been living in Europe, I have never for one day watched a telecast on the beautiful and luxurious scenery of Victoria Island in Lagos, Nigeria. All that the media concentrate on beaming to the viewers are criminal hideouts, bad roads, slums, dilapidated infrastructure, poverty, wars, famine, drought, etc.

There is this vexatious misrepresentation of Africans in the media - they don't tell success stories from the continent of Africa. All the bias and stark prejudicial practices create a social divide between the natives and African migrants. It further alienates the Africans from being accepted into the mainstream of society of the host country.

Enough is enough. If there is not attitudinal change, the gap between the haves-the natives, and the have nots - African immigrants, will grow uncontrollably.

HEALTH

Diseases associated with poverty, such as tuberculosis, which were supposed to be eradicated decades ago, are creeping back into black minority ethnic (BME) communities. Cases of HIV and AIDS among heterosexuals is far higher within certain African communities as are the incidences of sexually transmitted diseases. There are not only inequalities in health problems, they also exist at points of referral and treatment. Black patients were more likely, by as much as 40%, to be detained under the mental health act.

The law is failing to make a real impact on race equality. In the eyes of a large number of Africans in the diaspora, the glass is not half full, it is still half empty as far as health care dispensation is concerned. Only recently, after a very, very long battle and struggle, President Obama of the USA has just marginally won the mandate to implement the health care policy proposal that would benefit the millions of uninsured African - Americans.

CHAPTER NINE

Dispensation of Justice as it Affects Africans in the Diaspora

In the diaspora, often times there are different strokes for different folks. The justice system vis-à-vis Africans, leaves much to be desired. I wrote a critique against the Nigerian late maximum dictator, General Sani Abacha which was published by Newsweek International magazine in its September 16, 1996 edition yet my political asylum application was blatantly rejected by the Netherland Immigration and Naturalisation Department. (IND).

Black Africans are five times more likely to be stopped and searched than the whites. Judicial sentencing by judges and magistrates are often skewed against black Africans. They hand down sentences that are not in proportion to the crimes. Below is a short story that was carried by the London *Independent Newspaper* on Wednesday 5th September, 2007 - it was a damning report of judicial bias even against an African minor from Nigeria:

When Damilola Ajagbonna first sat down in a British classroom ten years ago, his thick Nigerian accent earned him the nickname "fresh off the boat". While in the playground, he was shunned because he did not own a tennis racket. But Mr Ajagbonna, now 19, was determined to succeed and in 2006 he was offered a place at Cambridge University to study social and political science. Today Mr Ajagbonna, described by a judge as a remarkable young man, faces being forcibly deported to Nigeria because he was six weeks late claiming British citizenship under immigration rules for children.

My critique of Gen. Sani Abacha's administration in Newsweek International Magazine

The decision has perplexed those who have watched him emerge as a model citizen. At the same time, immigration experts say his plight highlights the injustice and arbitrary nature of the law. For Mr Ajagbonna, the revelation that his new home regards him as an illegal immigrant is heart breaking. His father deserted his mother, who suffers from sickle cell anaemia, when he was a child in Nigeria. In 1999, his aunt decided to give him the chance of a new life in Britain.

"I have come to love this country. But when you discover that the country doesn't love you it is very upsetting- even more so when I have done nothing wrong" he said "It feels that my life has been taken away from me". Paul Sutton, his former head teacher at the Greig City Academy in Hornsey, North London where Mr Ajagbonna achieved 13 GCSE's and 3 A levels, said that he is one of the schools greatest achievers. "He has been our head boy for as along as I can remember, an absolute star who has given his school unfailing support".

Mr Ajagbonna's talents have been recognised by the United Nations which in 2005 appointed him an advisor on youth issues to UNICEF. He was closely involved in one of the flagship community projects run by the former Department for Education and Skills and has played prominent roles in the Children's Rights Alliance for England. At school he helped draft an anti-bullying policy and acted as a mentor to black students.

One of the judges who heard his case said "I find the appellant's contributions to youth culture in our society as a whole, and to his school society in particular, remarkable. He is clearly an outstanding young man". The asylum and immigration tribunal ordered the home office to review his case again, but it came to the same conclusion saying that it was not enough for Damilola simply to show that he was a "good chap" to stay in the UK. Do you know that if Ajagbonna were a white boy from Mexico or the Phillipines, his case would have been treated positively. But his ethnic origin has caused disfavour against him. Aside the Ajagbonna case, and according to European newspaper - European Voice of 24-30 January, 2008 page 4 - the European parliament has now agreed on a maximum 18 months detention period for those being returned home and a five year ban on re-entry to the European community.

Across the Americas, Europe and rich Asian countries, the judicial systems leave much to be desired in the ways they adjudicate cases that involve Africans in their respective continents. Judicial decisions are dispensed to favour the status quo, i.e. the national interest. Immigration laws, family laws, municipal laws, business laws, etc are drafted to suit the natives first, and foreigners last.

IMMIGRATION LAWS

The current system across America and Europe is the adoption of credit point immigration policy. I can say that without any fear of contradiction that this policy is designed to weed out as much as possible a lot of would be Africans who want to travel abroad.

As a result of this arrangement, most of the visas are now being issued to favour Indians, Chinese, Thais, Pakistanis, Malaysians and the Bangalis. They are far more preferred to Africans. When you query the reasons for this loopsidedness, they retort that they are better with information, communication and computer technology knowledge. Even Africans that have residency permits have to struggle and contend with long periods of waiting before their children, spouses or relatives could be allowed to join them. Procrastination is the norm across all the embassies when it comes to dealing with Africans' requests to travel abroad. And I continue to ask, when can we Africans overcome the double minority of being black and Africans.

FAMILY LAWS

Family laws are drafted to protect white families. When it comes to protection of the rights of children, they are more serious with the white children. Broken homes and single motherhood is now an epidemic among black communities abroad. Family dislocation is a bye word among black African communities in the diaspora. Family dislocation results in truancy, disobediance, bullying, etc. among black children of school going age.

BUSINESS AND EMPLOYMENT LAWS

Whites have better chances when it comes to doing business and getting the right jobs. They secure loans and are given grants without any strings attached and also without any overbearing administrative bottlenecks. To make matters worse, white people rarely patronise black African businesses as they do to themselves.

When it comes to employment opportunities, black Africans are the last to be hired and the first to be fired. Their chances of promotion on the job are very slim. Promotion glass ceilings are often imposed on Africans in the diaspora irrespective of their intelligence and input into the job.

MUNICIPAL LAWS

When it comes to accommodation, for example there are some property owners African migrants dare not go to rent apartments from just because he or she is a black African. This attitude can be stopped by the authorities. The town councils can redress that situation, they can but believe you me, they prefer to look the other way. The authorities know that some councils flout equality and diversity acts, yet they do not bring any of the erring local government councils to justice.

When it comes to elections there is general apathy and disenchantment among the African communities. They believe that participating in local elections would never make any difference to their lives. They feel alienated, and are not electable. They do not vote or stand for elections.

EDUCATION LAWS

In some countries across Asia, Europe and America there is outright segregation policies practiced against black Africans. There are some schools for instance in the UK where white pupils and students are pulled out if the school population is dominated by black children. Sooner or later you will find white parents sending their children to all white schools.

The governments are well aware of this scenario, yet there is no legislation put in place to check it. Many of the black African children are often abandoned in non performing schools or educational institutions which are inevitably dominated by African children. Because of the poor condition of educational delivery, they can hardly achieve the requisite GCSE grades that can qualify them to gain admission to study at higher institutions.

As a result of this situation, many African children complete their education without any prospects or opportunities to progress further. Scholarships and bursaries are awarded to children of natives to study while black African children are left out on account of poor performance. The white kids have surplus resources at their disposal to pursue their educational goals to logical conclusions. Lack of financial resources, emotional and psychological support in black families creates half baked graduates among black African children.

CHAPTER TEN

Shortcomings of Being an African in the Diaspora

Africans in the diaspora are straight jacketed. They are stereotyped as second class citizens, under achievers that are prone to crime. They are perceived to be violent and a race with a lower Intelligent Quotient (I.Q). They are seen to be more likely involved in anti-social behaviors. This misconceptions and misrepresentations often conspire to limit their chances of advancement in any society they find themselves in abroad. As a result of this, their self confidence is damaged. To make up for this unjust misrepresentation and stereotype, they resort to vengeance against the society. The authorities feel that their presence makes the society unsafe and as a result, they authorize incessant stop and search by the police.

Black people are six times more likely to be stopped by the police than white people. They are also six times more likely to be given a custodial sentence than whites, and are more likely to be refused bail and tried in crown courts. Africans are likely to be acquitted because in most cases they should not have been charged in the first place. In the Diaspora, schools do not reflect the ethnic make-up of the catchment area. There are a lot of smart black kids who are not getting into the best schools.

I think of the idea of black kids having to take extra lessons in whiteness so that they can handle going to a white school.

Too many Africans lack confidence, support and opportunities to live their dreams. Talent should be colour blind. Many Africans in the Diaspora are highly talented but being black African brings a barrier to progression.

There is discrimination against black Africans on the housing list because there is favour to the indigenous white families. Racism within the criminal justice system has created a crisis among black African communities by criminalizing young black men. Africans are snared by the justice system. Punitive sentences are doled out to African men. Africans of all ages are three times more likely to be arrested than white people.

Poor parenting and government failures characterize African youths. They take solace in dealing and consuming hard drugs. As a result of frustration, many do not exercise their civil rights for example, there is general apathy to politics. They will not vote and they have no idea who the key politicians are. When you query them why there is general disenchantment to civic duties, they say African votes do not really count and it does not make any difference. They also complain that African voters are the most disenfranchised, the most likely to be uninsured, they are the population that is suffering from substandard housing and poor education.

AFRICANS PERISH AS THEY FLEE TO ABROAD

Disturbing photographs of African immigrants who died as they tried to realise their dreams of a new life in the Diaspora, cover front and back pages of European newspapers. Many perish as they flee ravaging wars, persecutions, prosecutions, communal conflicts, family strifes, etc. The caption accompanying one picture in the *Daily El Mundo* a Spanish newspaper of 22nd May, 2007 reads - "they are not sleeping, they are dead". The pictures showed a group of West African immigrants who died in a small kayak trying to reach the Canary Islands, possibly from cold, hunger or thirst. They may have been wearing the clothes of others who died before them in the same tiny boat, but whose bodies were hauled overboard to make room for those who were still alive. Publication of the photographs followed a promise by the Spanish authorities to crack down on illegal immigration and the repatriation of more than 750 Africans, including 30 children, who were caught trying to enter the Canary Islands. Almost 600 of them were Senegalese.

West African Immigrants who died on their way to Canary Islands.

The Independence newspaper of Monday 28th May, 2008 reported that on the Island of Lampedusa, 27 young men from Ghana, Nigeria, Cameroon, Sudan and other countries, narrated their boat ordeal. As their flimsy boat from Libya floundered adrift for six days, two fishing boats failed to rescue them. The Maltese boat eventually allowed them mount the walkway but refused to have them aboard. One report by Spanish security service claimed that in 2005 up to 1700 migrants from Mauritania had died at sea. But the charity "Andalusia Human Rights" put the number far higher at 7000.

At least 300 people were dead and about 30 missing on the 3rd of October, 2013 after a migrant boat caught fire while crossing from Africa to Europe, prompting an outcry in Italy and calls for urgent action by international community. The 20 metres (66ft) vessel is believed to have sailed from Misrata in Libya two days earlier, carrying mostly Eritreans and Somalis. The boat was believed to have been carrying between 450 and 500 passengers. The boat's motor was believed to have stopped working, causing water to come into the vessel and prompting the passengers to set fire on a small piece of cloth to attract the attention of passing ships or rescuers. But fuel had mixed with the water flooding the ship, and the vessel caught fire.

Once the fire started, there was concern about the boat sinking and everyone moved to one side. As passengers fled to one side of the boat, causing it to flip, up to 500 people on board were flung or forced to jump into the sea. The passengers were just half a mile from the shore. The boat caught fire and sunk within sight of the Italian island of Lampedusa. They would have alerted the border police of the imminent danger if their phones were not seized by their smugglers. Passengers were barred from bearing mobile phones to avoid been detected by European coastal guards.

Since the passengers were not allowed to be with their phones they could not call any one for help. Many of the victims, who came from arid inland regions, could not swim. Asked on Italian radio what help was needed, Pietro Bartolo, Chief of health services for Lampedusa replied, "Coffins,

Coffins, Coffins and hearses." Gius Nicolini, the island's Mayor said "it is horrific, like a cemetery".

The UN secretary general, Ban Ki Moon, said the tragedy should be a spur to action. Pope Francis in an impromptu remarks, added: "The word disgrace comes to mind. It is a disgrace. It is hard to see how the flow could be curbed, with so many people so desperate for a chance to make a new life in the diaspora, and traffickers in so many ports ready to take their money."

In Britain, border checks have been tightened considerably since 2001 when the home office was rocked by pictures of illegal migrants massing at the Sangate camp near Calais ready to make a final bid to reach Britain. They feel that un-controlled immigration risked damaging poor communities and would put pressure on schools and housing.

The shortcoming of being a black African, by extension Black African-American in the diaspora resonated when George Zimmerman the killer of a young black African-American, Trayvon Martin was freed on Saturday night the 13th of July, 2013. Zimmerman capitalized on Florida's controversial **"STAND YOUR GROUND LAW"** to shoot dead Trayvon.

Mr Zimmerman, then 28, killed 17 year old Trayvon on the evening of 26 February, 2012 at The Retreat, a gated com-munity on the outskirts of Sanford in Orlando, Florida. On the night in question, Mr Zimmerman, a resident of the Retreat was driving through the neighbourhood when he spotted Trayvon. The unarmed teenager was walking home after buying a soft drink and a packet of skittles at a local convenience store. Zimmerman called the police, claiming Trayvon was behaving suspiciously but before the police arrived he confronted the youngster and fired a shot from his 9mm handgun. The teenager, who studied aviation and dreamed of becoming a pilot or an engineer, died from a single gunshot to the heart.

Trayvon Martin   George Zimmerman

He was originally released without charge but after a public outcry a murder probe was launched. Civil rights leaders argued that the half Peruvian, Mr Zimmerman targeted Trayvon who had no criminal record because he was black. In the night of Saturday the 13th of July, 2013 a six member jury took a decision.

Retreat was driving through the neighbourhood when he spotted Trayvon. The unarmed teenager was walking home after buying a soft drink and a packet of skittles at a local convenience store. Zimmerman called the police, claiming Trayvon was behaving suspiciously but before the police arrived he confronted the youngster and fired a shot from his 9mm handgun. The teenager, who studied aviation and dreamed of becoming a pilot or an engineer, died from a single gunshot to the heart.

He was originally released without charge but after a public outcry a murder probe was launched. Civil rights leaders argued that the half Peruvian, Mr Zimmerman targeted Trayvon who had no criminal record because he was black. In the night of Saturday the 13th of July, 2013 a six member jury took a decision.

The six strong jury included five white women and another woman of undisclosed ethnicity. The jury returned a not guilty verdict. Zimmerman was found not guilty of killing an unarmed black teenager and was also acquitted of lesser manslaughter charge.

Protests sparked off in San Francisco, Philadelphia, Chicago, Washington and Atlanta. Flags were burnt. In Oakland, California gangs of youths attacked police and set cars on fire while others smashed windows in a downtown area. Zimmerman went into hiding immediately after the verdict. He was described as "a dead man walking" having received numerous death threats. President Barack Obama, who after the Florida killing had declared that if he had a son, " he would look like Trayvon", an appealed for calm.

In an effort to defuse tensions civil rights leader Jesse Jackson urged people to avoid violence. Fellow anti-racism activist Reverend AL Sharpton said the verdict was a slap in the face of African American people. Many celebrities took to Twitter to express outrage at the verdict. Singer Beyonce held a minute's silence at her concert in Tennessee.

Pop babe Rihanna, 25, also hit out at the decision to free Mr Zimmerman, saying it was the saddest news ever. Rap star P. Diddy, 43, voiced his outrage at the verdict, tweeting "George Zimmerman is free #not right # No Justice for Trayvon". The killing unleashed furious debate across the US over racial profiling and equal justice.

CHAPTER ELEVEN

Benefits Derived from Coming Back to Africa

Africans in the diaspora must all think of returning back some day. There is a popular saying that East, West, North, and South, home is the best. European Union and the United States of America and Canada committed themselves on the 10-11 April, 2006 to action to stem the brain drain which is damaging staff levels in African hospitals. Diplomats from European Union should discuss a possible EU code on "ethical recruitment". Its aim would be to ensure that European hospitals do not deprive their African counterparts of proper care by luring doctors away with offers of better pay and conditions.

According to the African Medical and Research Foundation in Nairobi, only 10% of physicians trained in Kenya's public hospitals each year, remain in the country. Malawi, where HIV infection rates among pregnant women are estimated at 15-20%, has only two doctors to every 100,000 inhabitants. I want to ask the emigrating African doctors why the mass exodus to abroad? Africa has all it takes and needs to train and retain the best and the brightest from Africa.

European Union, development aid earmarked for migration related projects should not be used to deal with security issues. The money should be reserved for education and healthcare in Africa. We have to promote good governance in Africa before people can think of returning back to Africa.

Governance is about reinforcing security, reaching the millennium development goals, addressing HIV and tuberculosis, providing education and health.

On 16th and 17th November, 2006 sixteen African heads of state and leaders of the World Bank and United Nations attended a conference on governance organised by the European Commission in Brussels. The conference focused on how states can be managed best and how to overcome the challenges of governance.

Paul Wolfowitz, the president of the World Bank and Mark Malloch Brown, the deputy secretary general of the United Nations, participated. The main themes for the conference included state rehabilitation after conflict, the role donors can play in governance. And also included in the themes are free press, policies to protect vulnerable groups and minorities, involving non-governmental organisations (NGOS) and fighting poverty.

We have to promote good governance in Africa before people living abroad can think of returning back to the continent. In my humble opinion, European Union funding is not enough to stop people wanting to leave the African continent. These African countries have to develop, investors must become interested. Europe must invest. Africans are poor because they do not have the means to develop their resources and economies. If people have nothing to eat at home, if they have no jobs, if they cannot support themselves, they will cross the borders to where they can live and eat and nobody can stop them.

Since advanced nations are complaining that economic benefits of immigration might be negligible and that this is putting a big strain on public services, African brothers and sisters have to think of returning back home with dignity. Africans face a lot of problems abroad. Over the past few years, Africans who have just arrived abroad and even many who were born in Europe and America, find themselves plunged into a brutally increasing internecine brand of ethnic warfare.

It pits group against group, race against race in competition for economic survival.

Already it is a clash of underclasses and underworlds. Why do they leave the African continent to suffer these problems? There are a lot of benefits struggling Africans living abroad can derive when they vacate Europe to live in their motherland. One of those benefits is freedom - freedom is the ability to express yourself without any fear and to choose between options for the ultimate good of the individual.

As an African in the Diaspora, you are often weighed down by so many laws and obligations to the extent that you are almost enslaved by it. You are not free, and are bonded and binded by strict rules and laws and regulations. But way back in Africa, the rules and laws are more endearing and compassionate. You are more free to do a lot of things without recourse to strict laws and statutes.

NO DISCRIMINATION- In Africa, we only experience a bit of tribalism but not to the scale of blatant discrimination as practiced abroad. You earn more respect among your kinsmen. If you want to do business you are offered loans and grants to boost your business with very simple conditions. Also in Africa, there is abundant land for investment - land is very, very cheap and affordable.

NO RACISM- Activities of Neo Nazis, Klu Klux Klan, xenophobic individuals, etc, surely increases incidents of racism in the diaspora. According to result of studies conducted on human health, racism causes high blood pressure among ethnic Africans. Living in an environment that is xenophobic, you feel unwanted and troubled. But back home we are black and proud of our ethnic background. We do not entertain any fear of humiliation and insult to our human dignity. We have the same Negroid roots - so back home nobody plays the race card because we are of the same race.

BENEFITS OF GOOD WEATHER

Two thirds of the African continent broadly lies within the tropics. Naturally, it is very warm throughout the year. The whole of Europe, United States, Canada and most part of Asia lie within the cold and chilly temperate weather conditions - so Africans living in the diaspora suffer from wintery and unhealthy weather conditions.

They experience almost on a daily basis wintery showers and fierce cold and disturbing winds. The Caucasian race do not need to acclimatise in their natural habitat - but the Africans do in order to survive. It is medically explained that consistent and prolonged exposure to extreme cold temperatures by black Africans could trigger high blood pressure, which in turn causes hypertension, type two diabetes and eventually heart attacks.

Nowadays, Caucasians relocate and move in droves to warmer countries across the world. If Caucasians fear the aftermath of continued exposure to extreme cold weather, what of the Africans? So brothers and sisters, please come back home because you will never pay to enjoy the available good weather conditions in Africa.

AFRICA MORE FAVOURED BY NATURE

Africa is blessed with abundant green sceneries and people are living very close to nature. In the diaspora, there is rampant problems of environmental pollution, orchestrated by industrialisation and heavy duty transportation. Cities are polluted and choked by carbon emissions. But in Africa, you are very close to nature. Besides deforestation problems, the African environment is ever green. Food and drinks are from natural sources. There is no problem of genetically engineered foods and drinks. Food crops are grown and harvested with little or no chemical input.

RICH CULTURE AND TRADITION

When one is in his/her natural and ancestral home in Africa, there is cultural and traditional affinity and fulfillment. The languages, mode of dressing, codes of greeting, etc. are tied to our cultural heritage. If you uproot yourself from this traditional setting, you will be like a fish out of water. We must all get back to our roots, as the famous musician, Lucky Dube, sang!

GOOD COMMUNITY SPIRIT

Africans are imbued with the spirit of philanthropy and humanitarianism. In Africa, you pop into peoples homes informerly, no protocol is compulsorily observed when dealing with one another. There is the spirit of camaraderie. We are not indifferent to one another's problems and feelings.

In developed countries nobody cares for one another, only the system cares. In Africa, one person's problem rubs on the other person. Joy and peace also rub on one another. Problems are communally solved. For instance, if somebody dies, every member of the community mourns. Also, people share in times of peace, festivities and joy without any restrictions. Neighbours are invited to compounds and courtyards to share and give to one another.

CHAPTER TWELVE
The Way Forward

The United States closed the 19th century with the declaration in Plessy versus Ferguson - that rigid segregation was the natural order. It was a time when W.E.B. Dubois wondered if America would ever get beyond its homespun apartheid. For centuries there has been the problem of the colour line, and the relation of the darker to the lighter races of men. Still the whole world enters the millennium self consciously striving to be a more tolerant place.

Immigration has been a useful tool for the whites in Europe, Asia and America to wield the big stick over persons of a darker hue to assert their authority. Racism is not human but sociological. Almighty God created us all differently, like beautiful flowers in a garden. It is our diversity which makes the human race the rich mosaic that it is with each culture fitting perfectly to the grand design. But black African asylum seekers find themselves in the front line of racist abuse and victimisation.

Europe and America in past times did have a reasonable humane reputation as far as asylum goes, but that only applies to white faces fleeing persecution from totalitarian regimes from Europe e.g. Jewish people. But nowadays the Hitlers and the Stalins of Europe are thankfully long gone. Most of the tyrants and rights abusers are now governments in African countries. But Africans fleeing away from these African tyrants are turned away because they are black or brown in their skin colour.

This concluding chapter has offered me the golden opportunity to voice my own opinion of racism as it affects Africans in the diaspora. Now more than ever before, Europe, America and developed countries of Asia, had descended heavily against migration from every other parts of the world in general and African immigrants in particular.

They blame migration for the unsustainable pressure it was placing on services. But for the advanced nations to stem the flow of Africans' migration, greater consideration should be given to the links between migration of Africans and European Union and United States of America's development aids. The EU, USA and Asian countries can't separate development policy for Africa from migration and economic policy. At the moment, a complex and often outdated patchwork predominates issuance of work permits. Quotas, student schemes and national immigration policies are often modeled on the need to restrict Africans from former colonies.

But they fail to realise that even in states of the EU, USA and Canada where there is low unemployment, there will be skills gaps and jobs that many of their citizens are unwilling to do. The World Bank has confirmed that African migrants send remittances to their countries of origin which far outstrip EU, USA, and Canadian development aids. Africans come to developed economies of the world for one overwhelming reason, to find work.

But they are worried that their society is being changed beyond recognition by migration. Whites accuse migrants especially African migrants of abuse of their hospitality by committing crimes and pushing hard and dangerous drugs. They claim that the addition to production African immigrants bring to their economies is exactly the same as the addition to population. So to deal with African migrants they use destitution as an instrument of policy. It is a deliberate tool to frustrate and push out African migrants.

Being a black African makes you ultra visible to the extent that shop assistants follow you around as you enter the store. Politicians across Europe, Asia and America had descended heavily against migration. They blame migration for unsustainable pressure it was placing on services. For this singular reason, the United Kingdom (UK) Tory leader had called for the minimum age for spouses moving to Britain to be raised from 18 to 21 years

In Switzerland in November, 2007 Mr Blocher, whose party now has its largest recorded majority in Parliament, ran an antiimmigration election campaign which depicted white sheep standing on a Swiss flag kicking a black sheep from their midst. He was quoted by the Swiss newspaper, Sontags Blick saying he fully supported the campaign "we must show Africans that Switzerland is not paradise". With integration primarily a matter for national governments, the European Commission has limited powers.

"We are not a country of immigration" Chancellor Helmut Kohl once said. And officials of his government endlessly repeated the phrase, as if the words could contradict the reality of the presence of foreigners in Germany's midst. Nazi fanaticism over ethnic purity triggered the horror of the Holocaust.

Citizenship is an important symbol of inclusion. But the biggest problem is that few Americans and Europeans see immigration as a process that enriches their societies.

They fail to realise that immigration makes up for these advanced countries' declining birth rates and also boosts their economies. They do not care about that - they are adamant. Frontex, the EU's border agency, has started its operations on the Canaries with Spain and Italy providing boats and planes for patrols. Frontex began co-ordinating joint patrols by EU member states off the islands. They work together to intercept boats leaving the coast of Africa.

Joint patrols have also included Senegal, Morocco and Mauritania whose beefed up border and marine patrols have largely cut off important routes used by people smugglers. Patrols in the Mediterranean started in June, 2007 to help stem the flow of immigrants to Malta and Italy. Frontex also has new tools to help it respond.

A European patrol network was established which will see member states coordinating patrols in EU waters to ensure better surveillance. Would - be immigrants have been put off by systematic expulsions from Spain. In a way, it is sending a strong signal. Before, the perception was that if you made it to the Canaries, you were sent to the mainland with a piece of paper saying you had to leave but then people disappeared into the informal economy. There is now increased surveillance.

EU countries, the Americas and Asia should take a cue from what has just happened in Ireland. A Nigerian who fled to Ireland as an asylum seeker, has become the country's first black mayor, in what is seen as a landmark in multicultural relations.

Rotimi Adebiri, who was elected Mayor of Portlaoise town council, received a standing ovation amid scenes of celebration. He declared - "This is not just a country of a thousand welcomes, but a country of a thousand equal opportunities." Elected by six votes to three, those councillors who voted against him apologised, citing party tradition. One of them said to him - "you seem to radiate happiness and joy".

Since life chances in the diaspora are determined to a very large extent by ones race, Africans should look inward and make the best that mother Africa has to offer. And to the countries in the EU areas (EEA), the Americas, Russia and the developed countries of Asia, they must improve efforts to end the imports of conflicts diamonds, timber, minerals, oil and stop the export of light weapons that fuel African wars which had forced a lot of Africans to flee abroad.

Africans can make the 21st century the African century. If we embrace democracy and empower the African citizens, we will be able to turn Africa's tremendous reserves of diversity and creativity into a positive force for the world as we have done with music and the arts. We have to put our houses in order by overthrowing corrupt dictators, establishing free market economies and moving forward towards democracy.

The African continent must be prepared to undergo a re-markable transformation after decades of stagnation and regression. The majority of its 750million people are now living under elected governments for the first time ever. There remain massive problems, from widespread poverty to the eruption of civil and regional wars, donor fatigue, dis-illusionment, racism and emerging market crisis.

The developed nations should allow African countries to be in charge of their own economies. If these problems are not ade-quately addressed, a lot more of our youths will migrate abroad where they will definitely face the harsh reality of racism.

Printed in Great Britain
by Amazon